Harbour Bridge Sydney Views

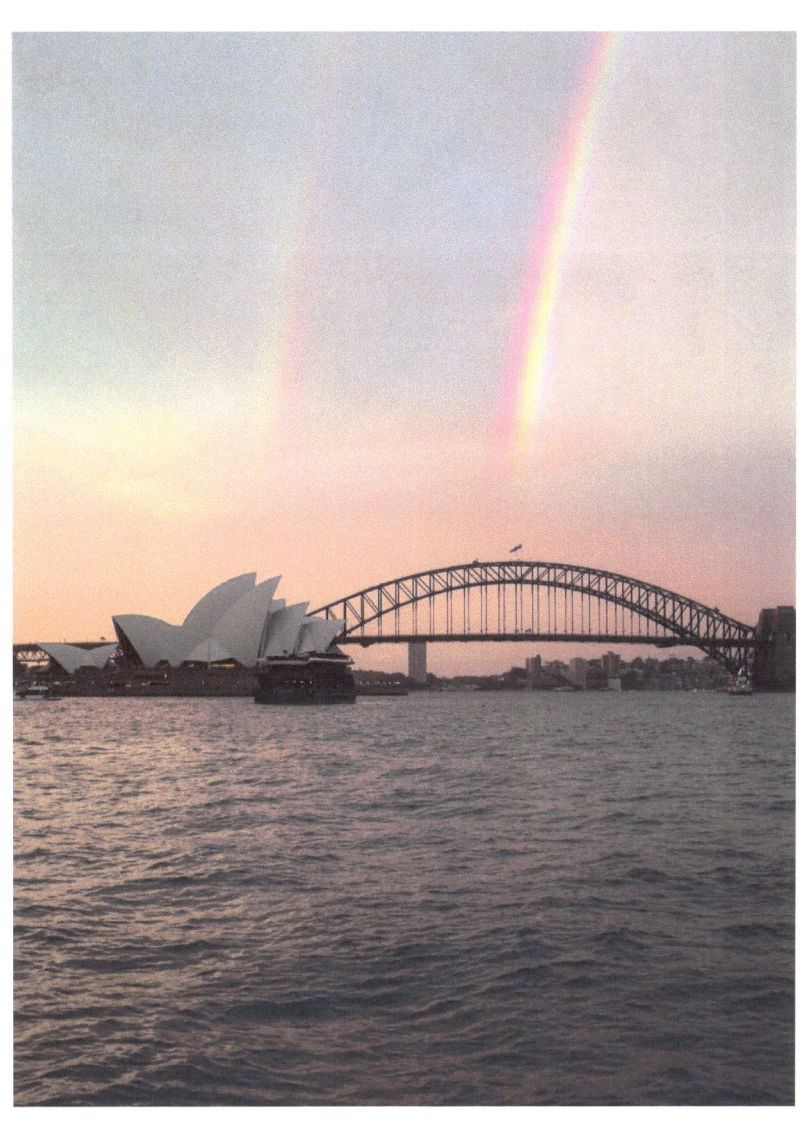

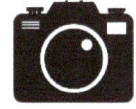

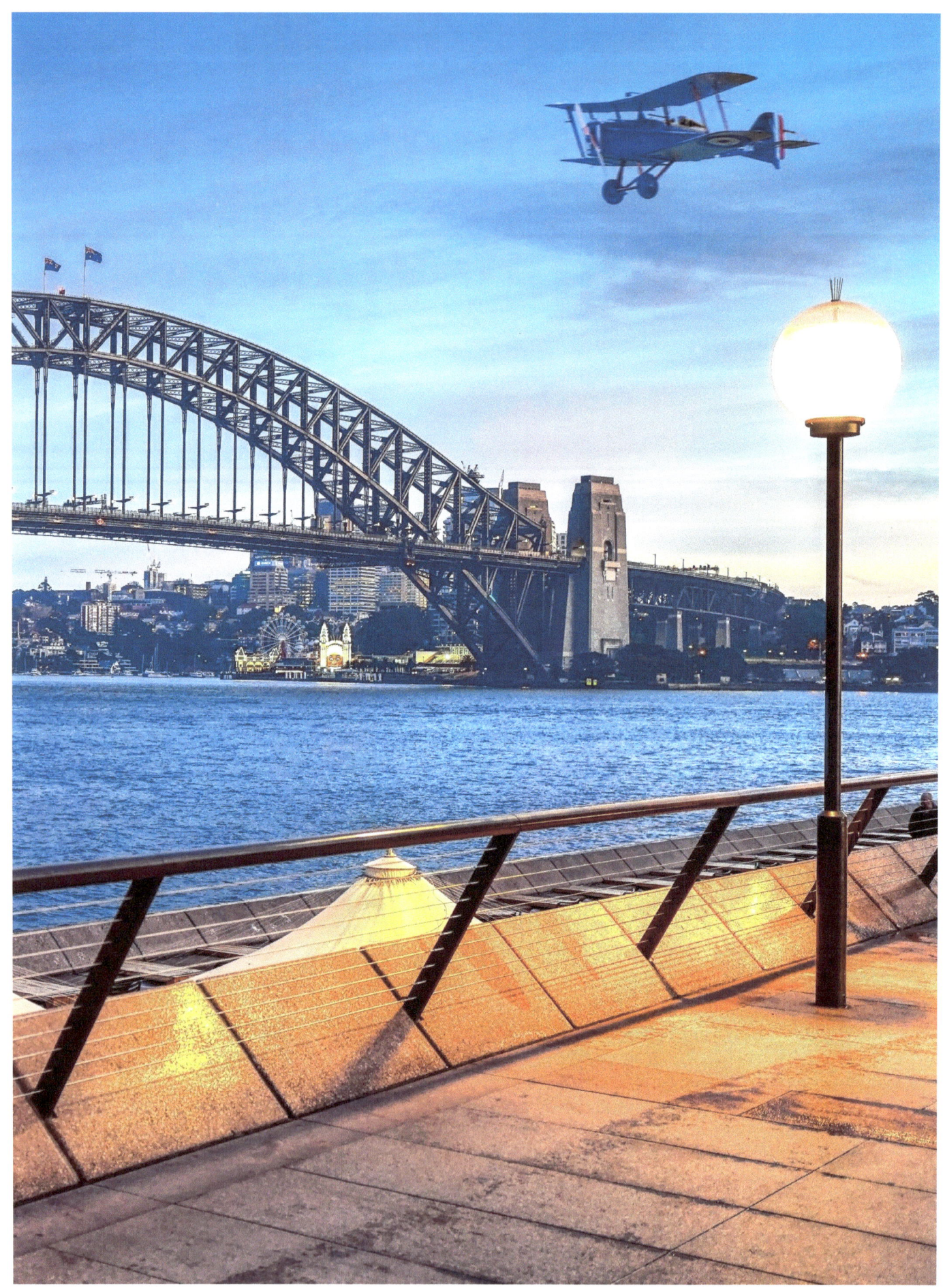

Bridge from Opera House – Philip Connor

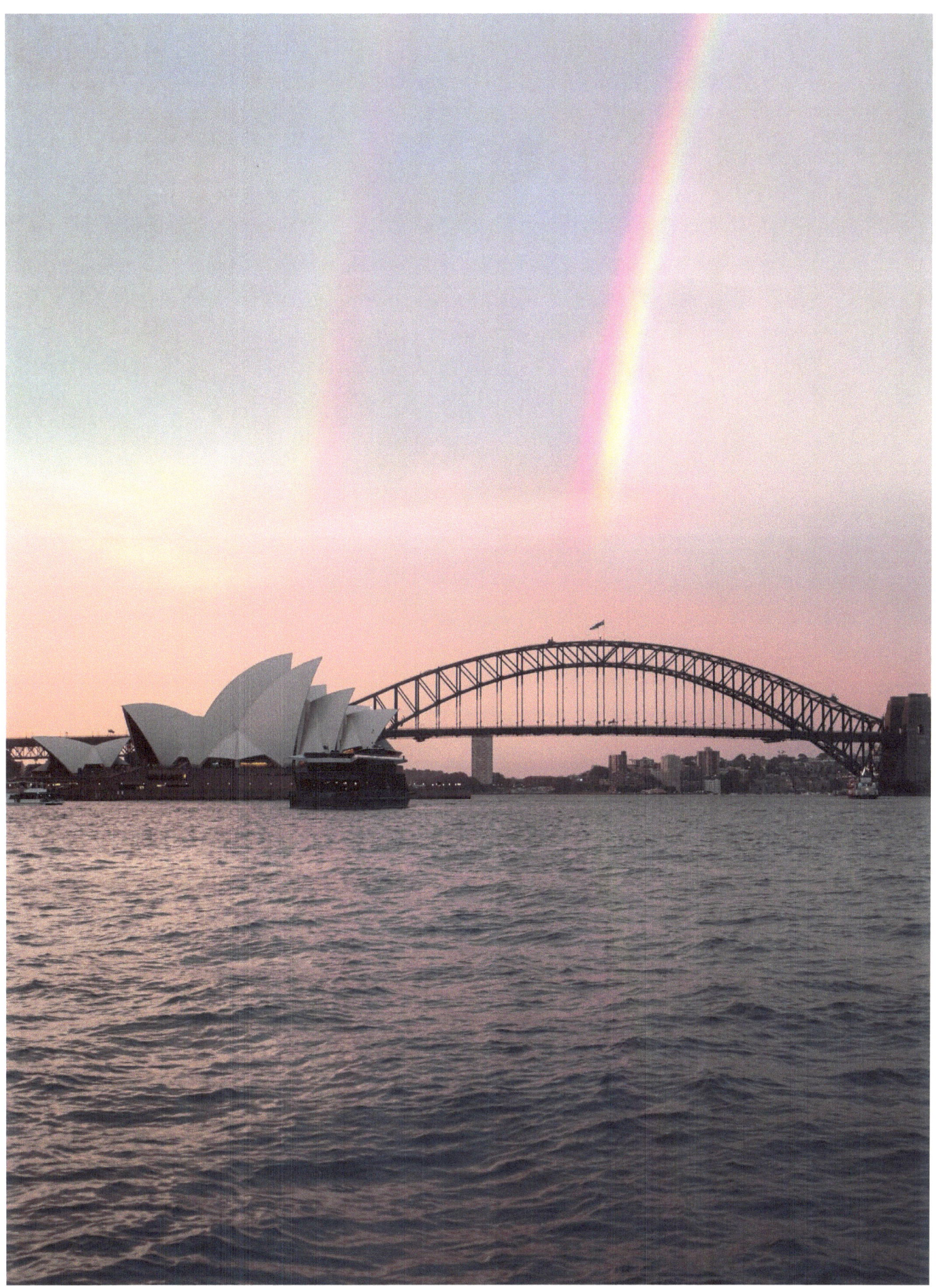

Late Rainbow seen from the Manly Ferry – Marley Clovelly

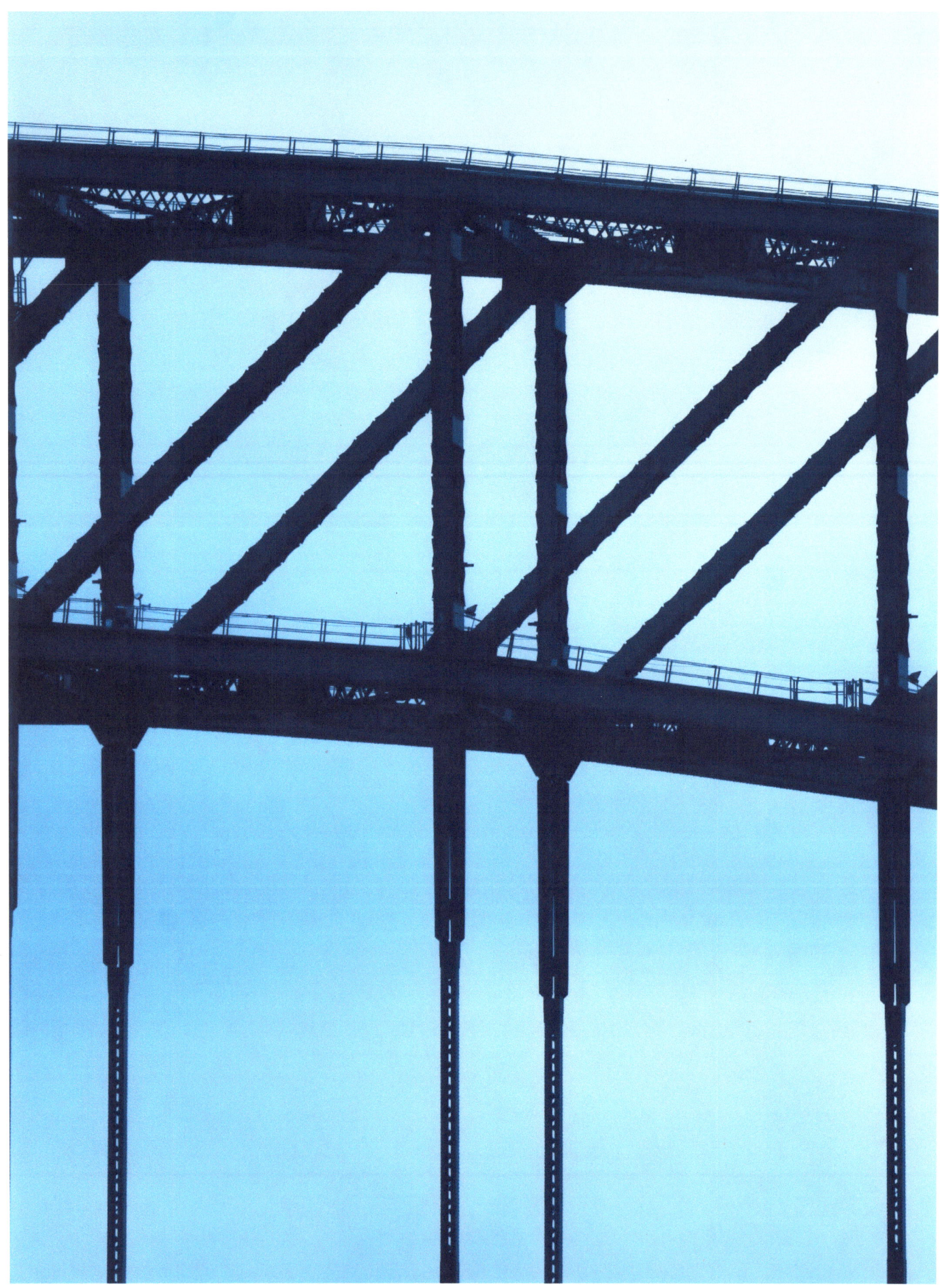

Maintenance Catwalk – Ben Mack

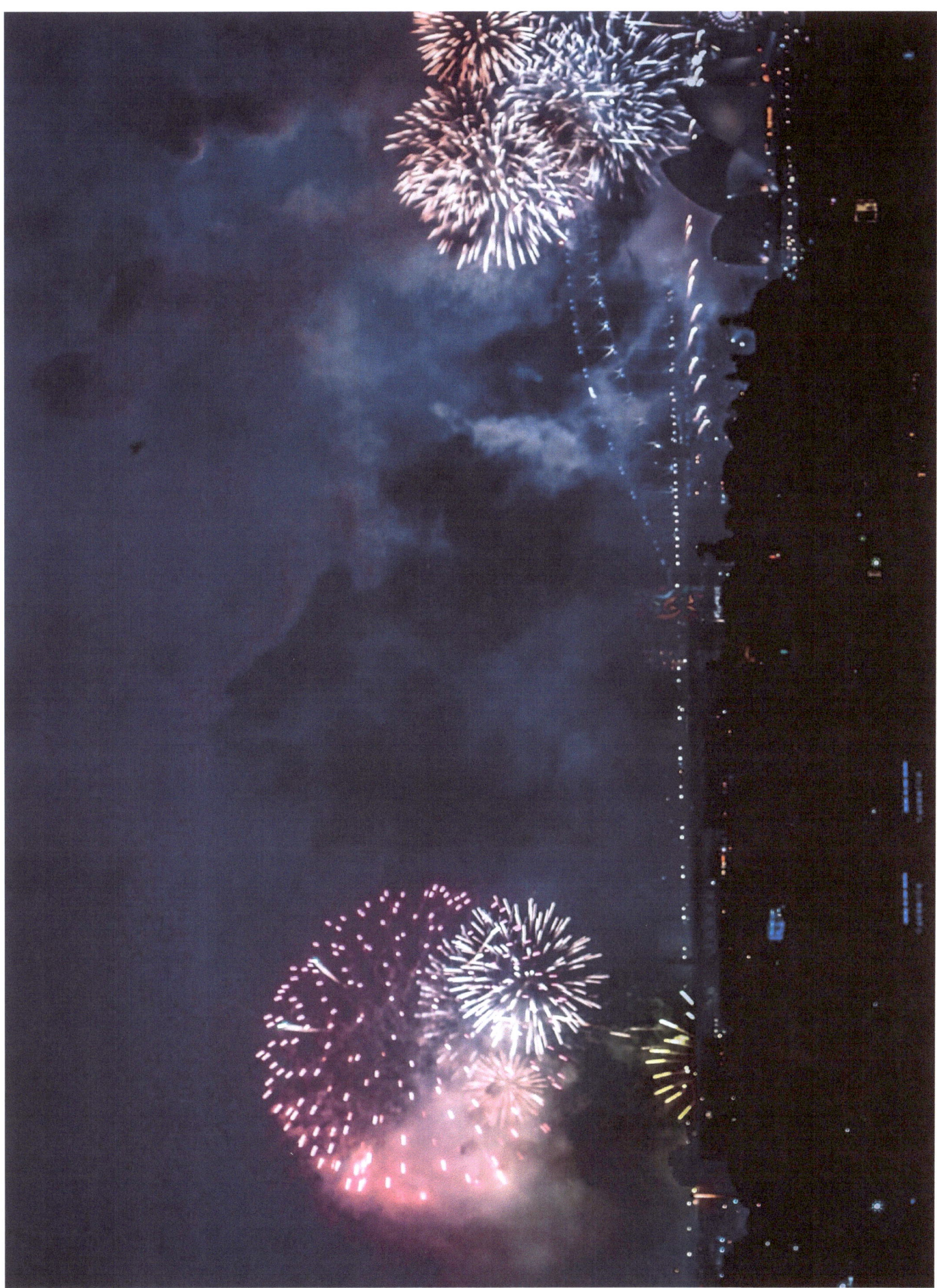

Fireworks New Year's Eve – Belle Co

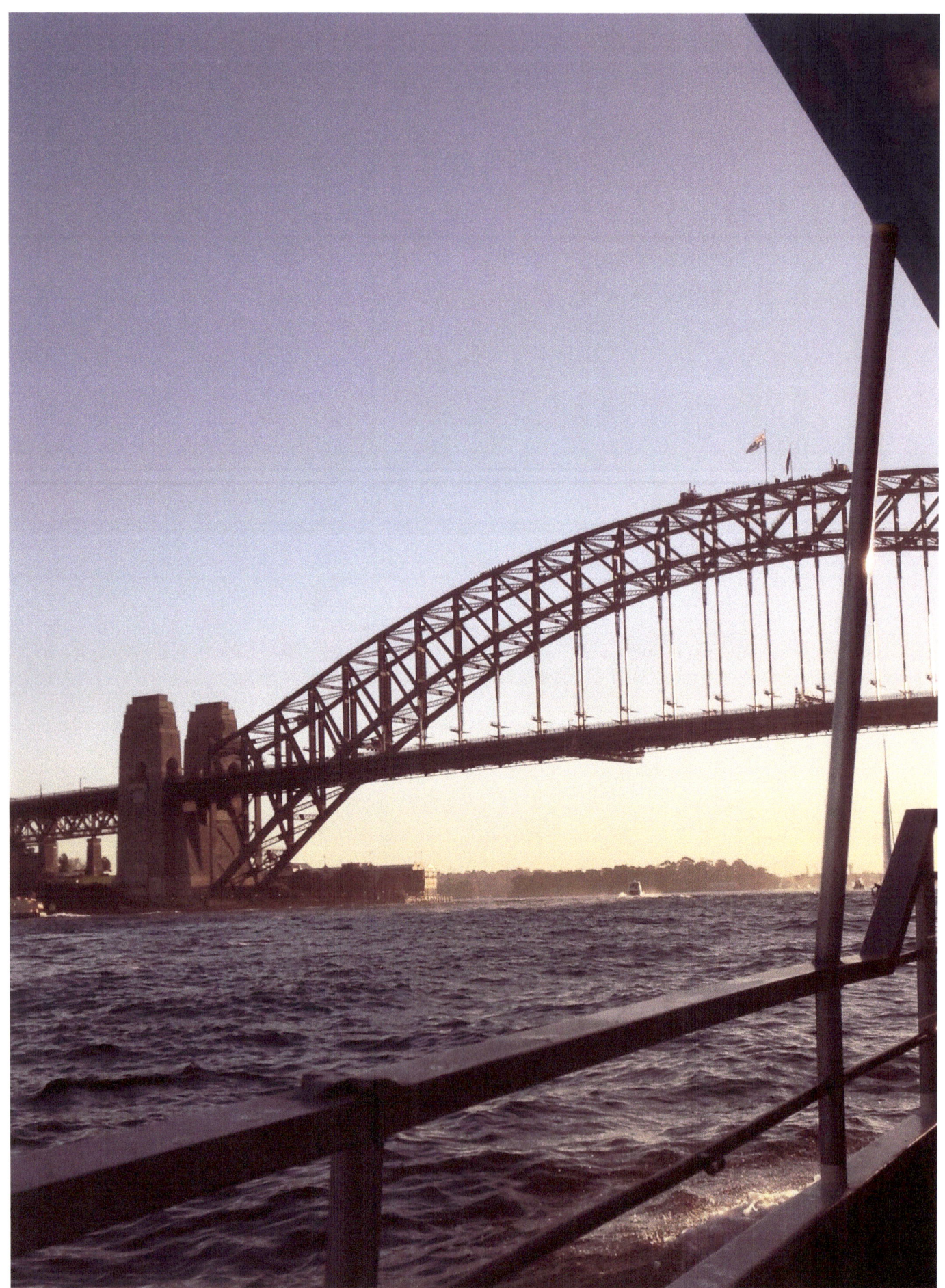

Returning home after whale watching – Carmel Duryea

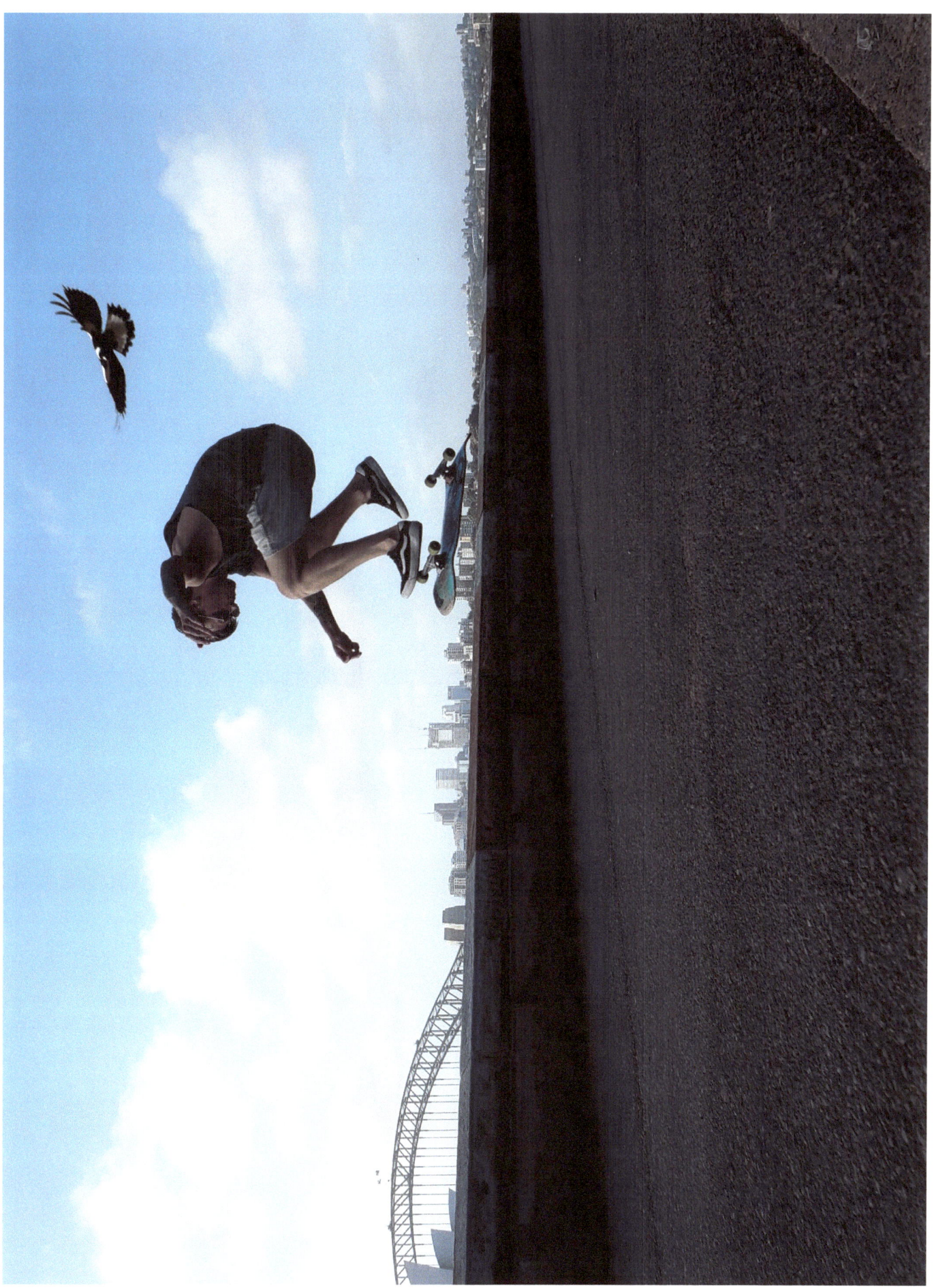

Skate for Your Life – Kio

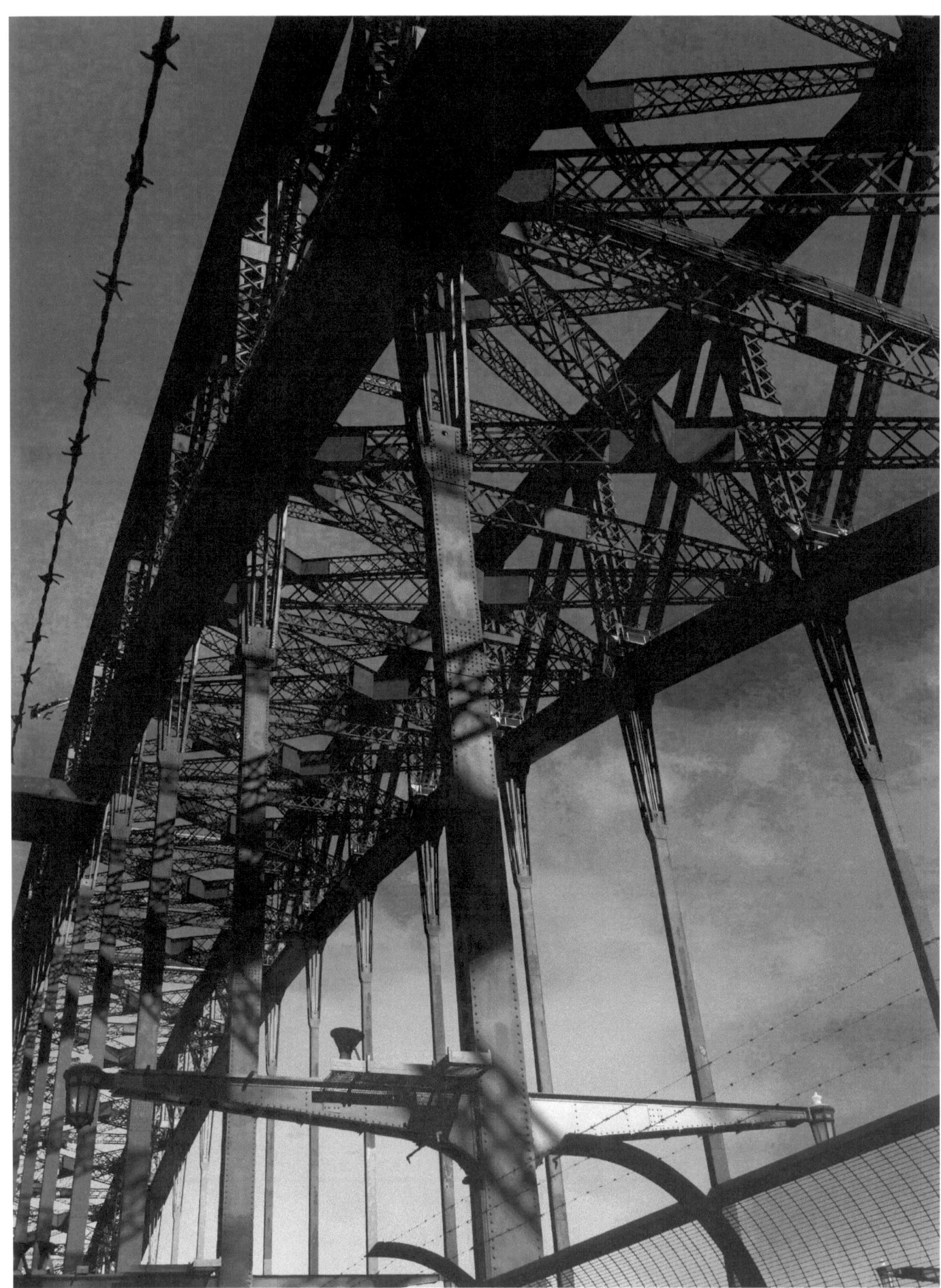
View from pedestrian walk as seen in 1936 – Carmel Duryea

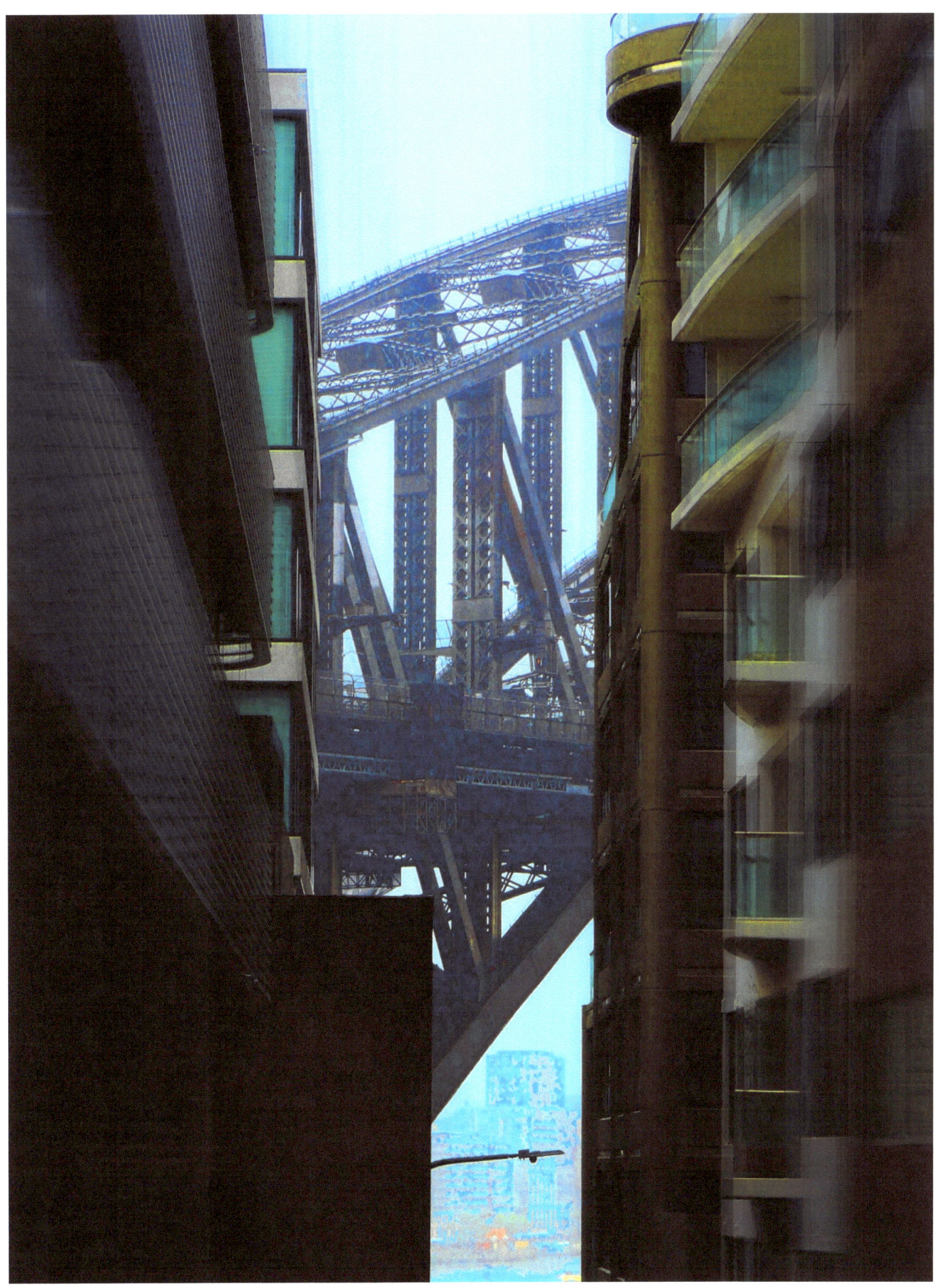

Office View from McMahons Point – John Koenig

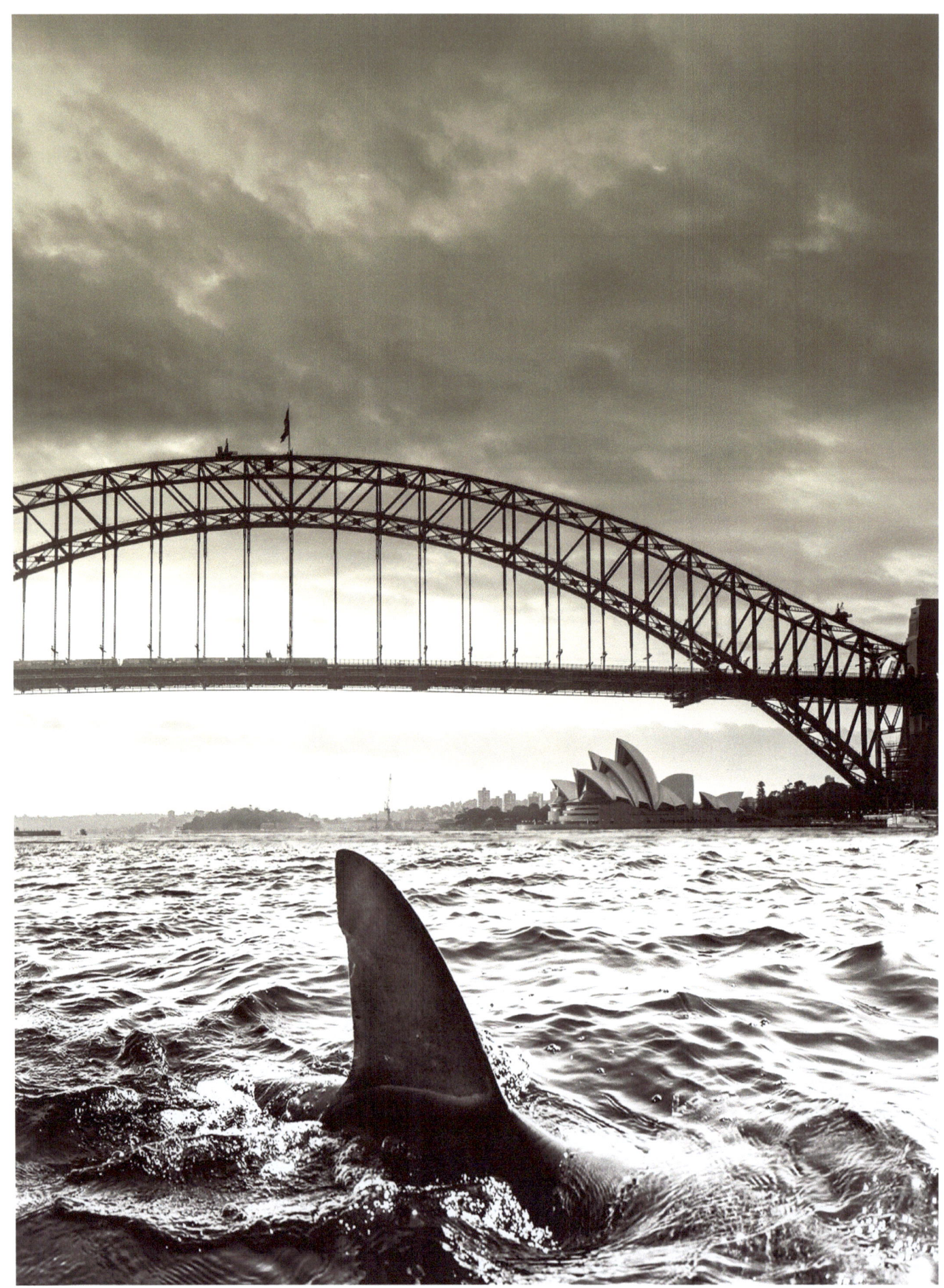

Shark 'n Sails – George Talbot

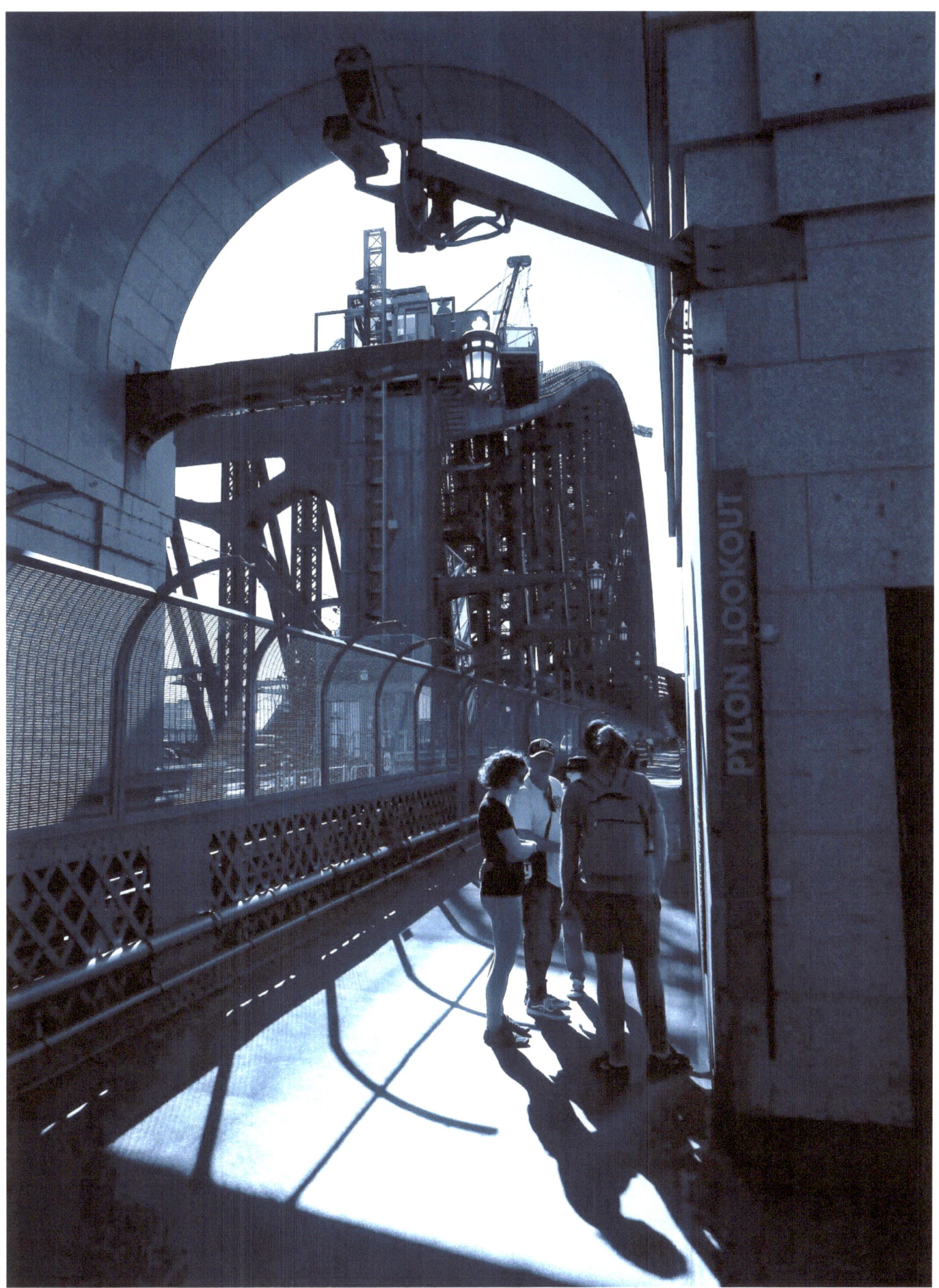

South East Pylon – Carmel Duryea

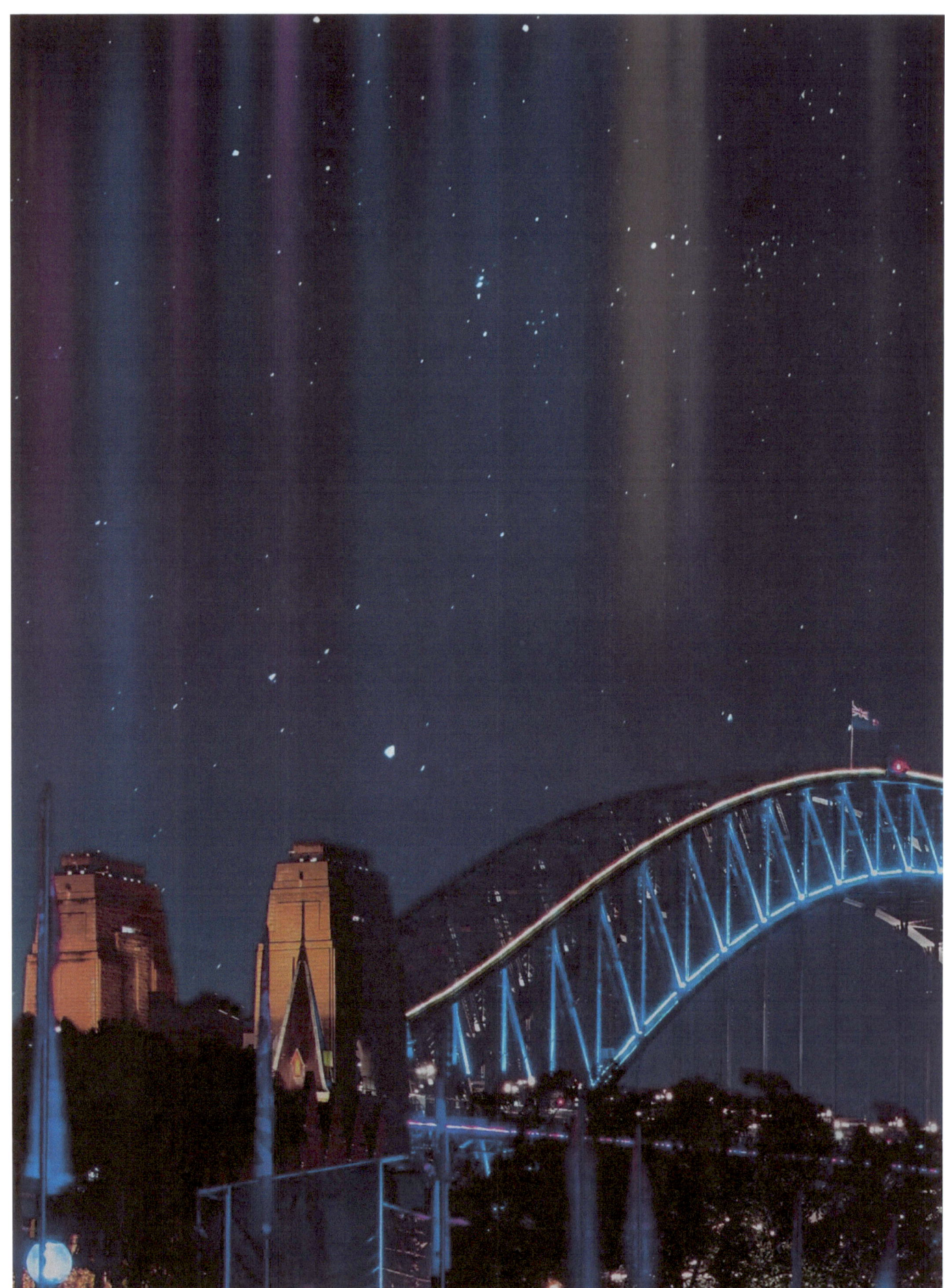
Night Bridge – Benjamin Sow

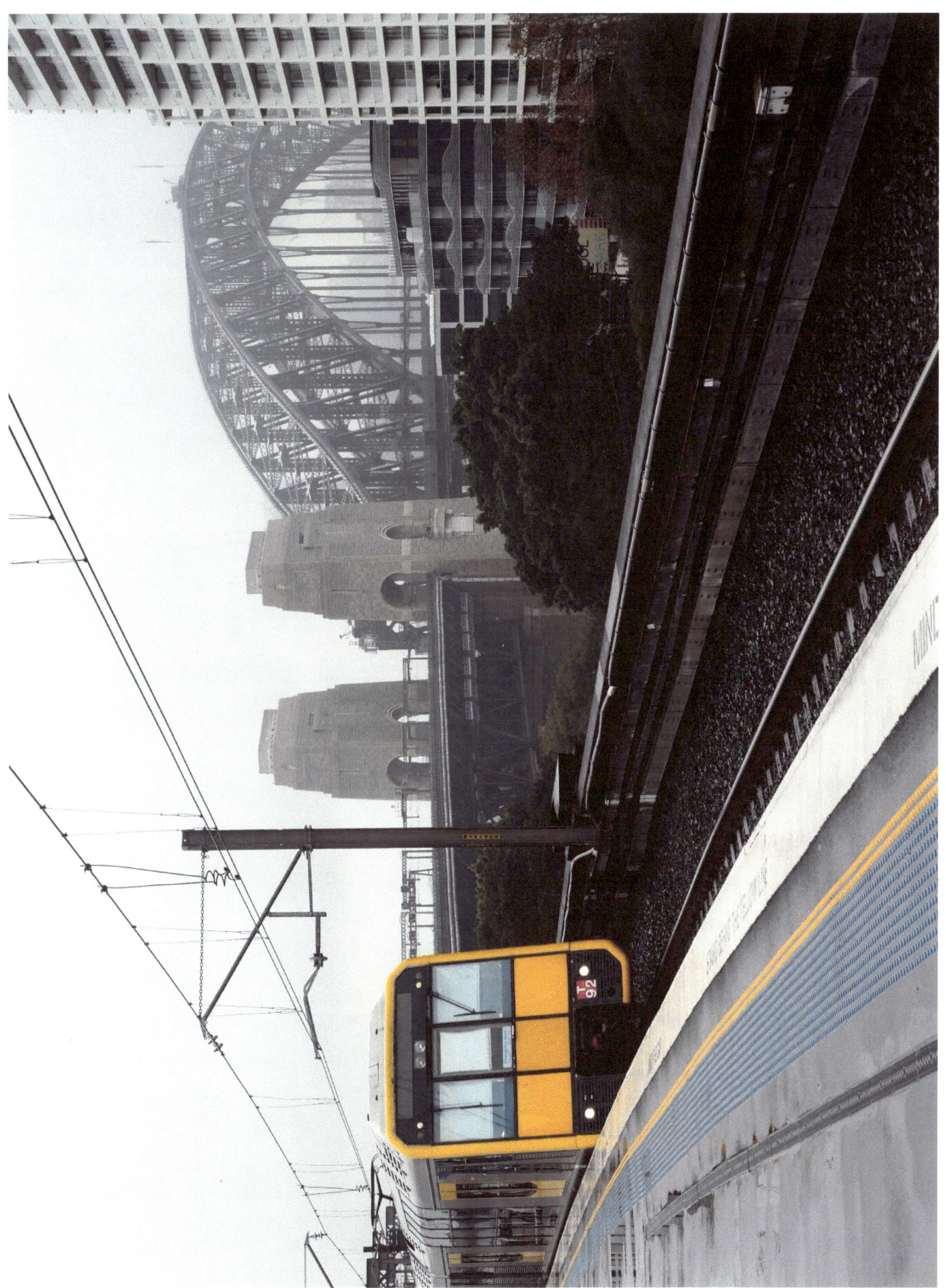

Wet Monday Morning at Milsons Point Station – John Koenig

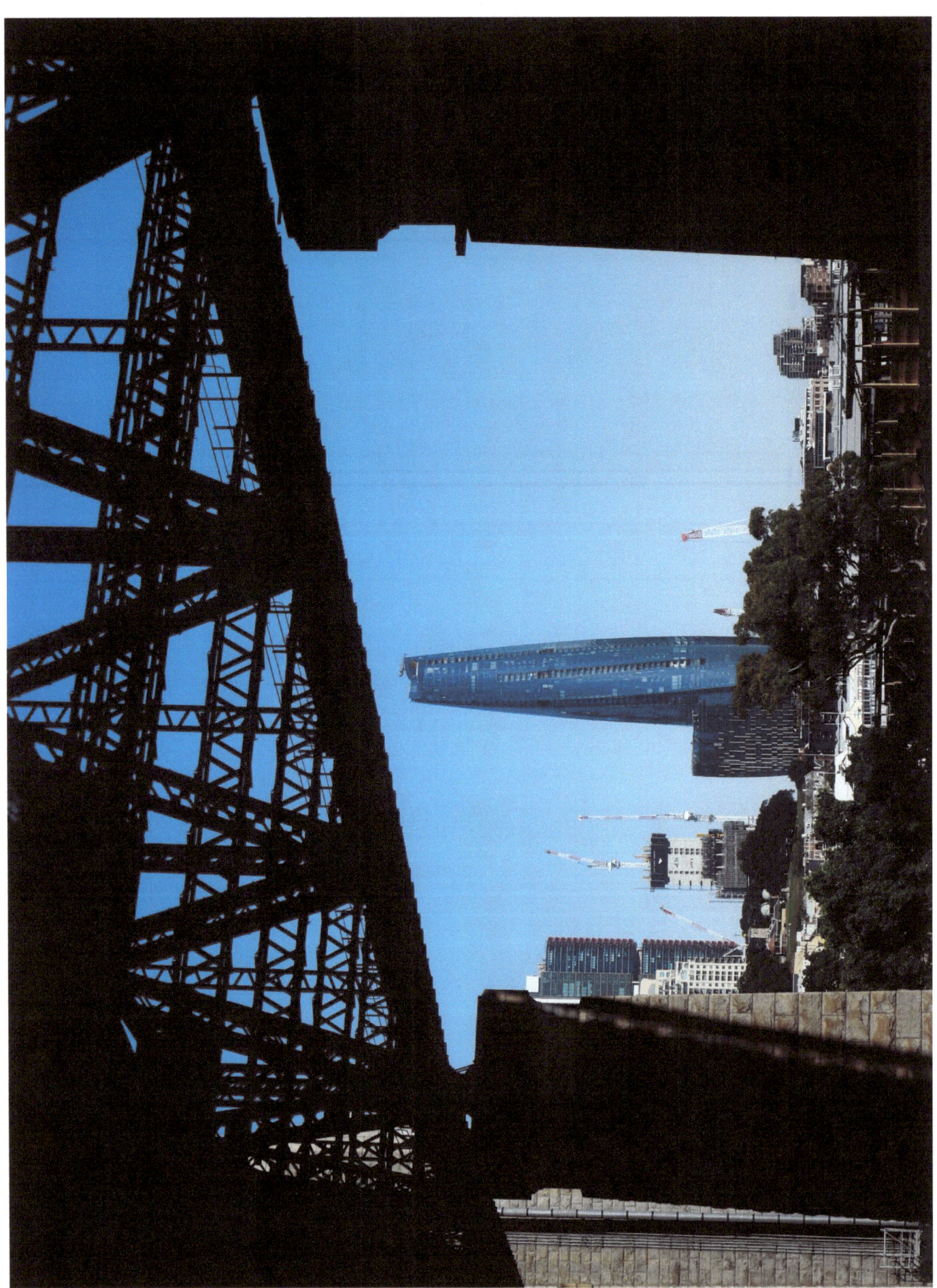

Underside Bridge View of Crown Casino Tower from Milsons Point – John Steadman

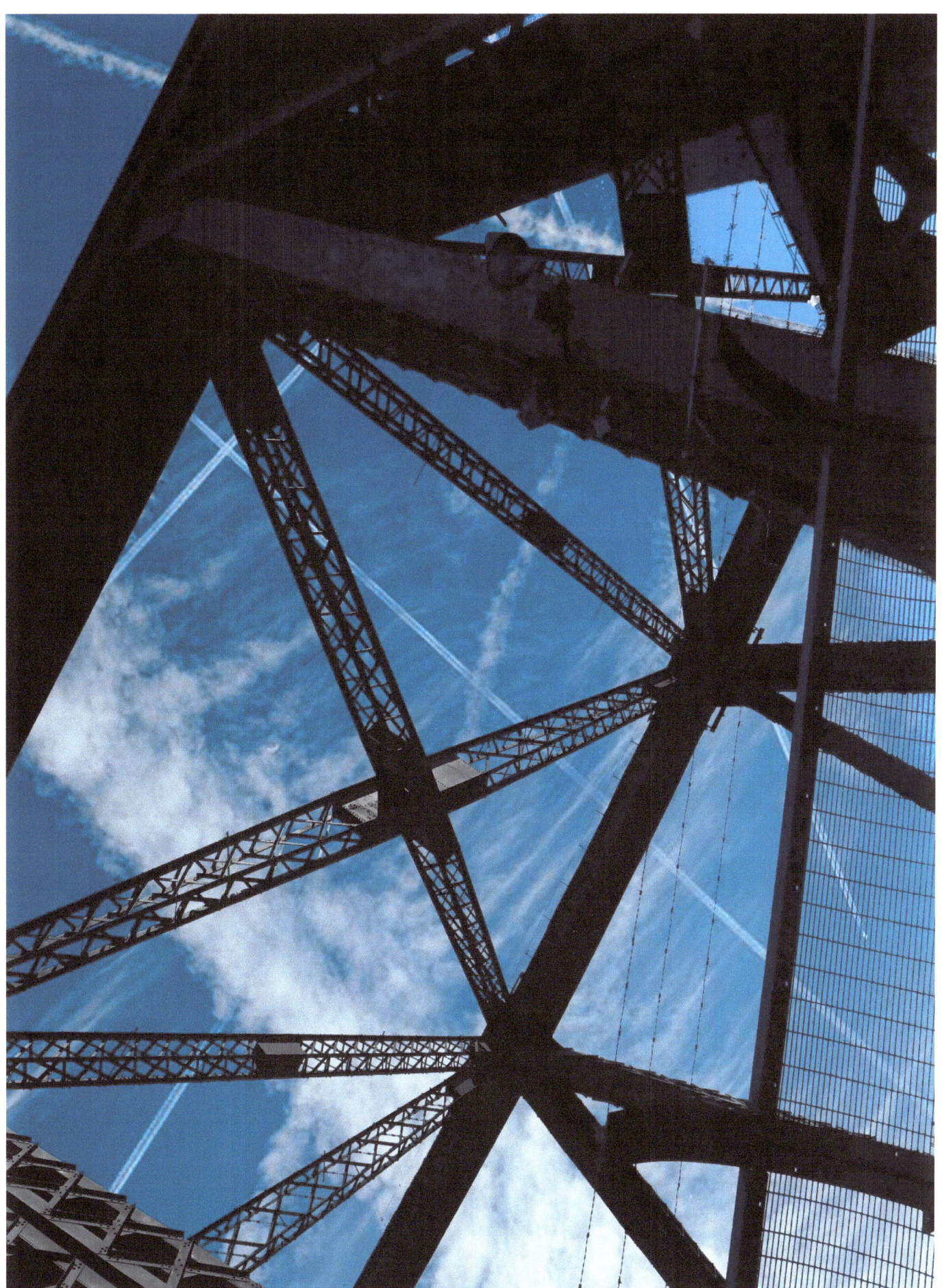

Through the Framework – Carmel Duryea

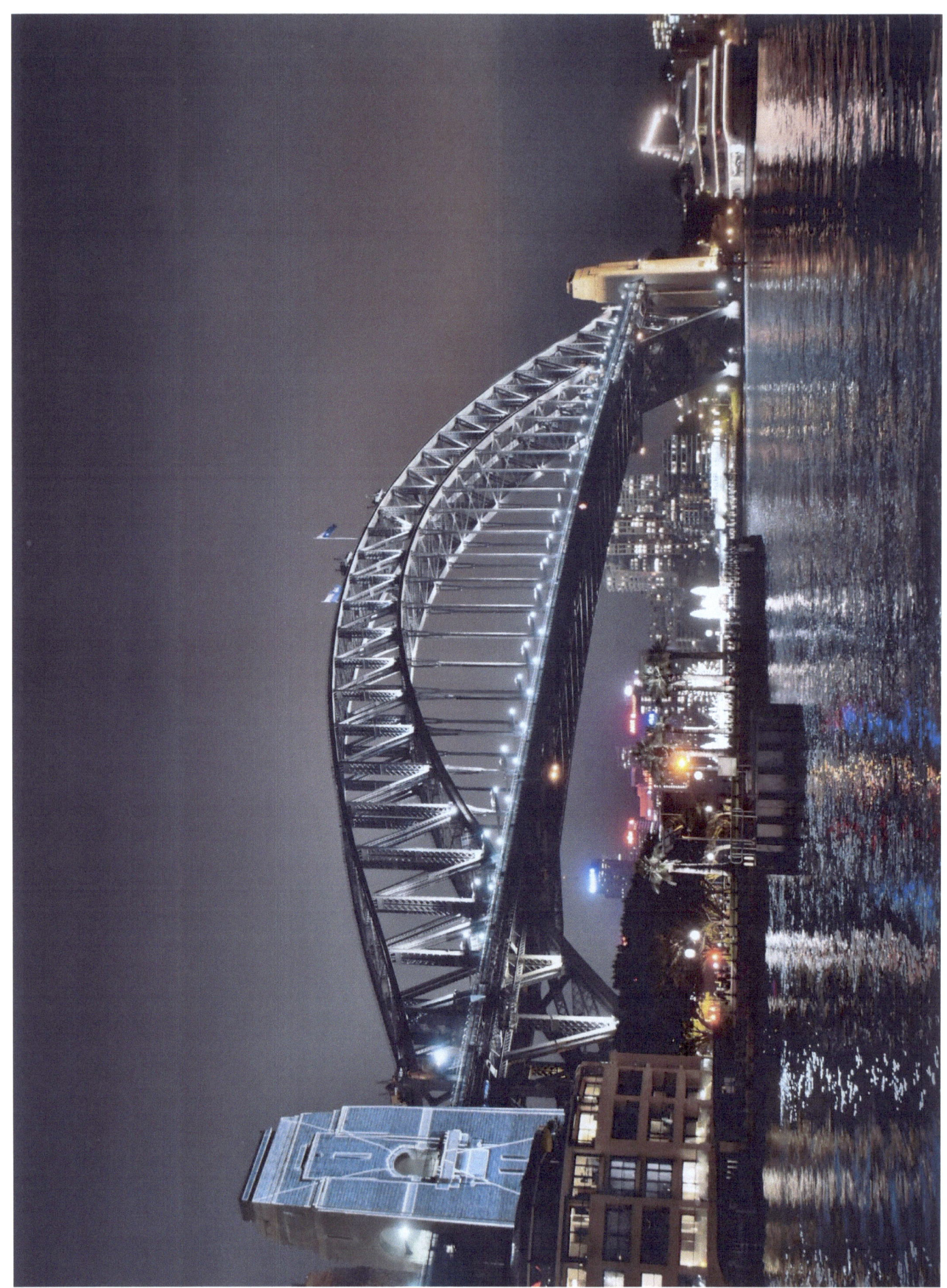

Lights amongst the Clouds – David Dibert

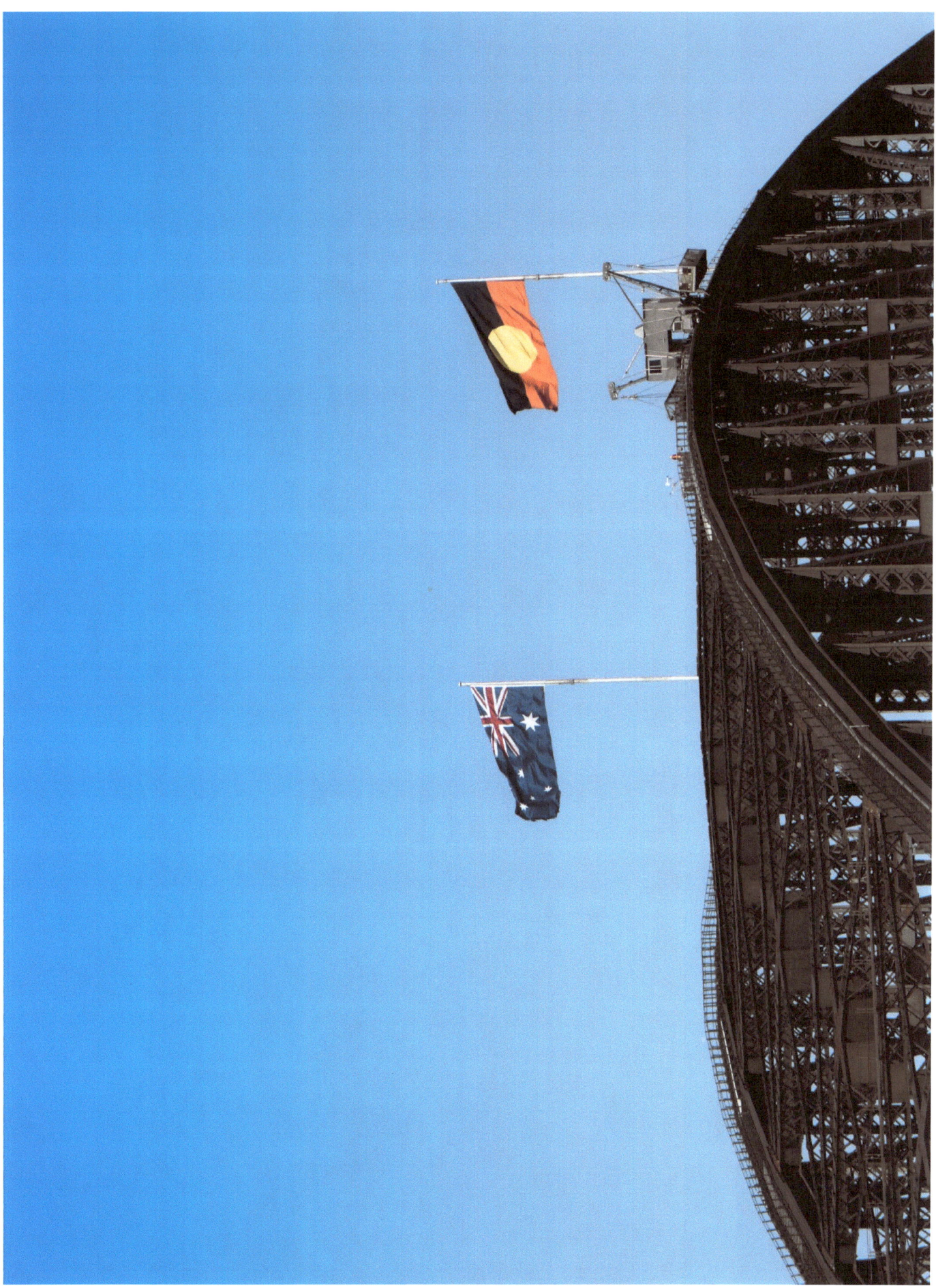

Dream for a United Nation – Karin Gottschalk

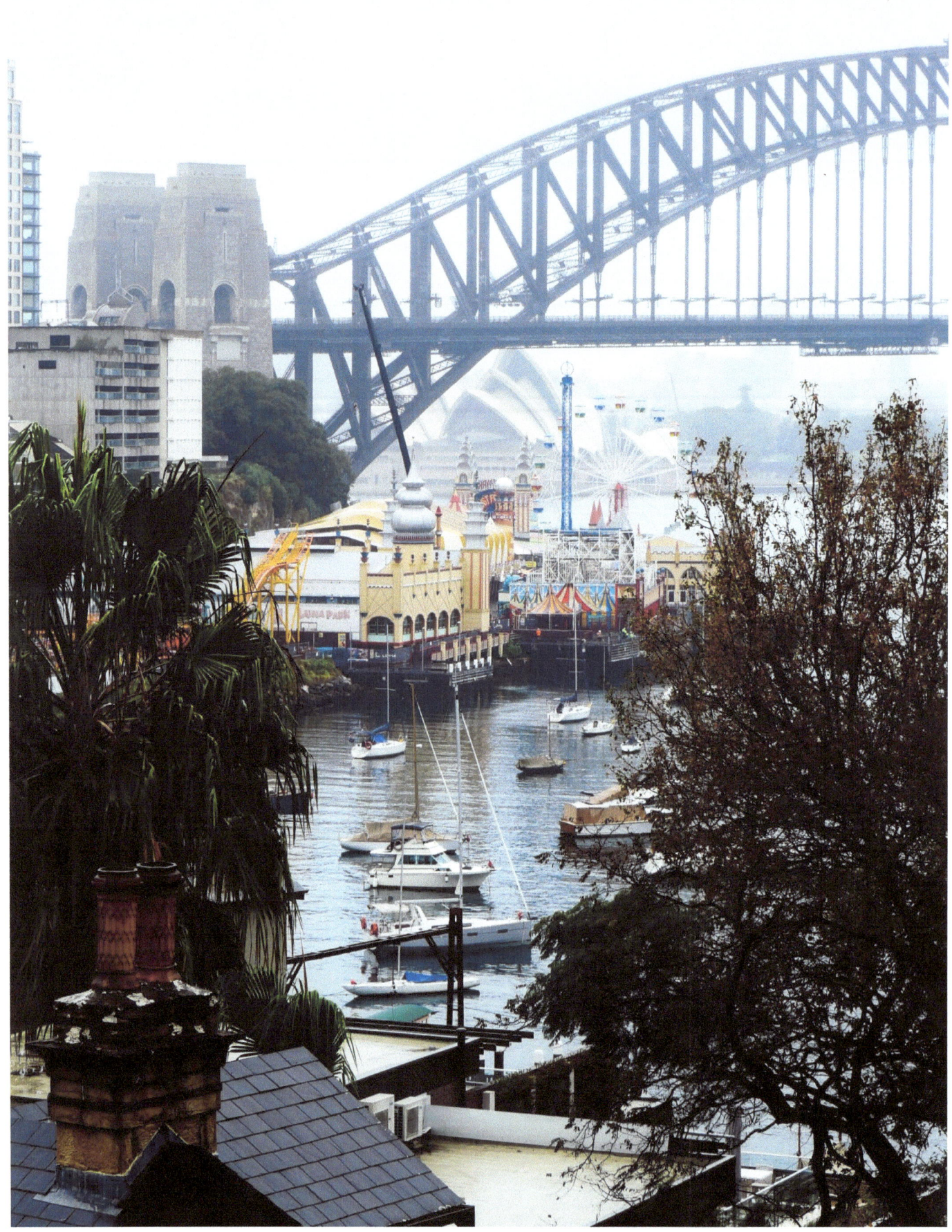

Colors on a Gray Day (Part 1) – Logan Five

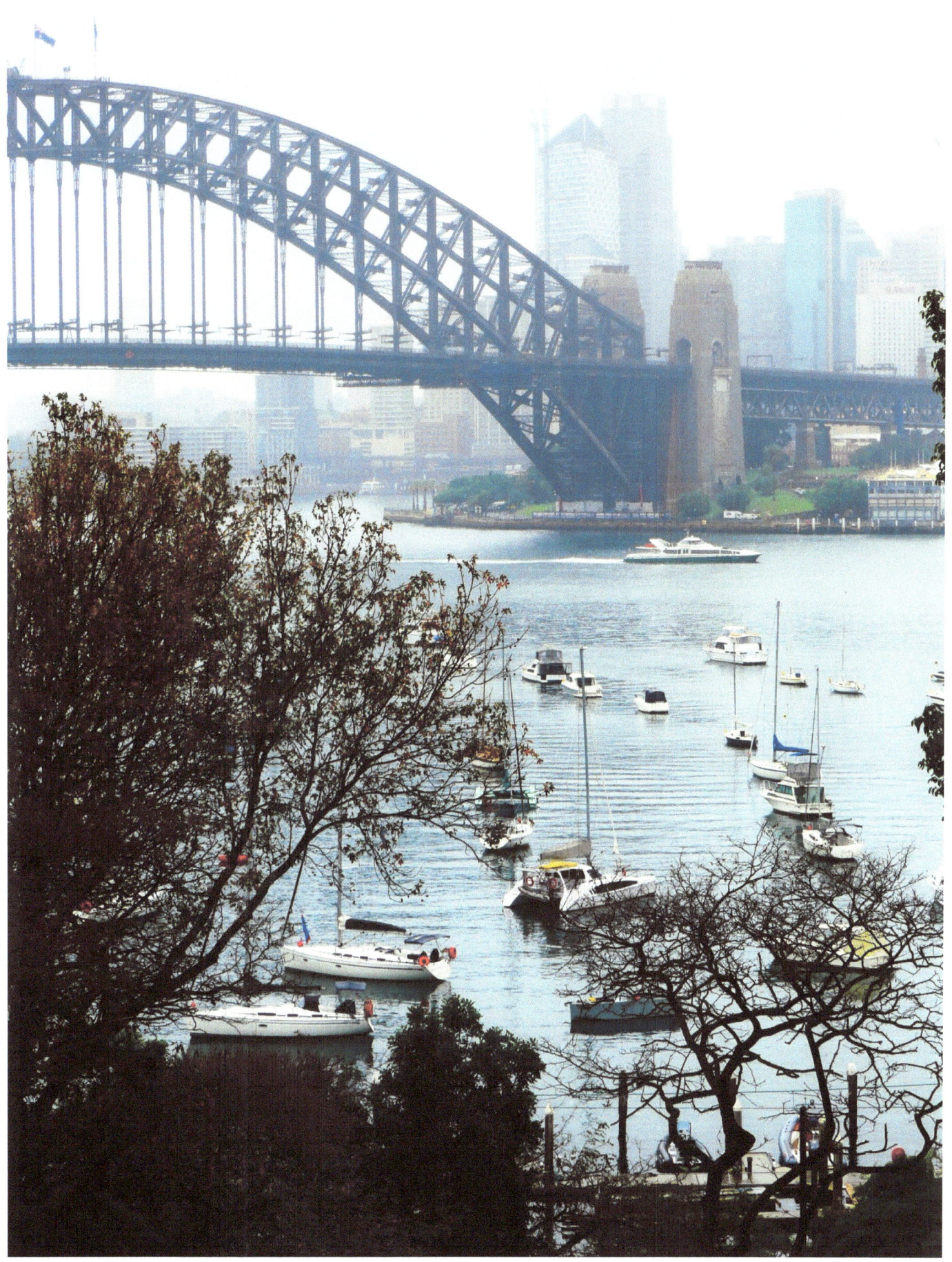

Colors on a Gray Day (Part 2) – Logan Five

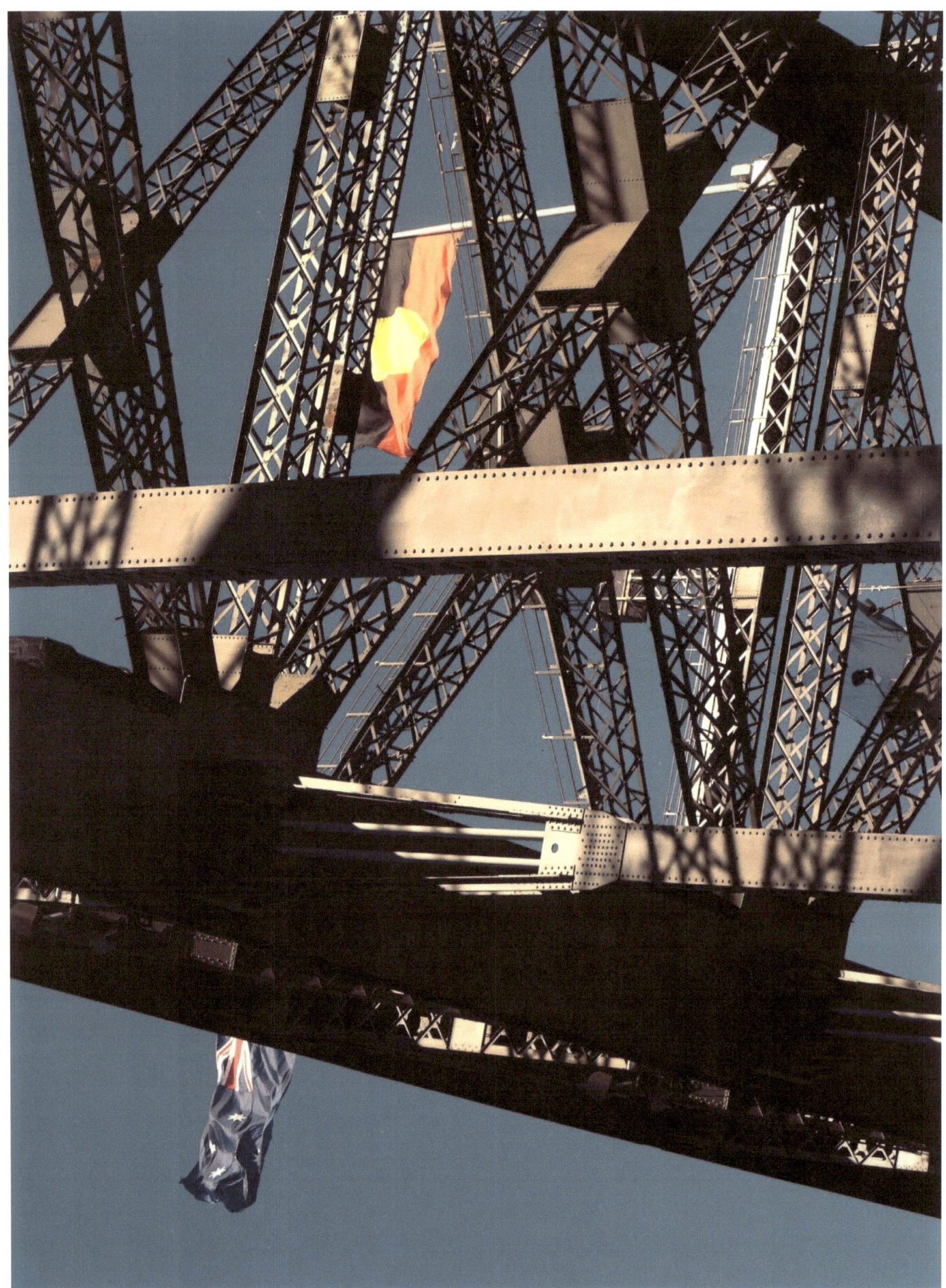

Two Flags United – Karin Gottschalk

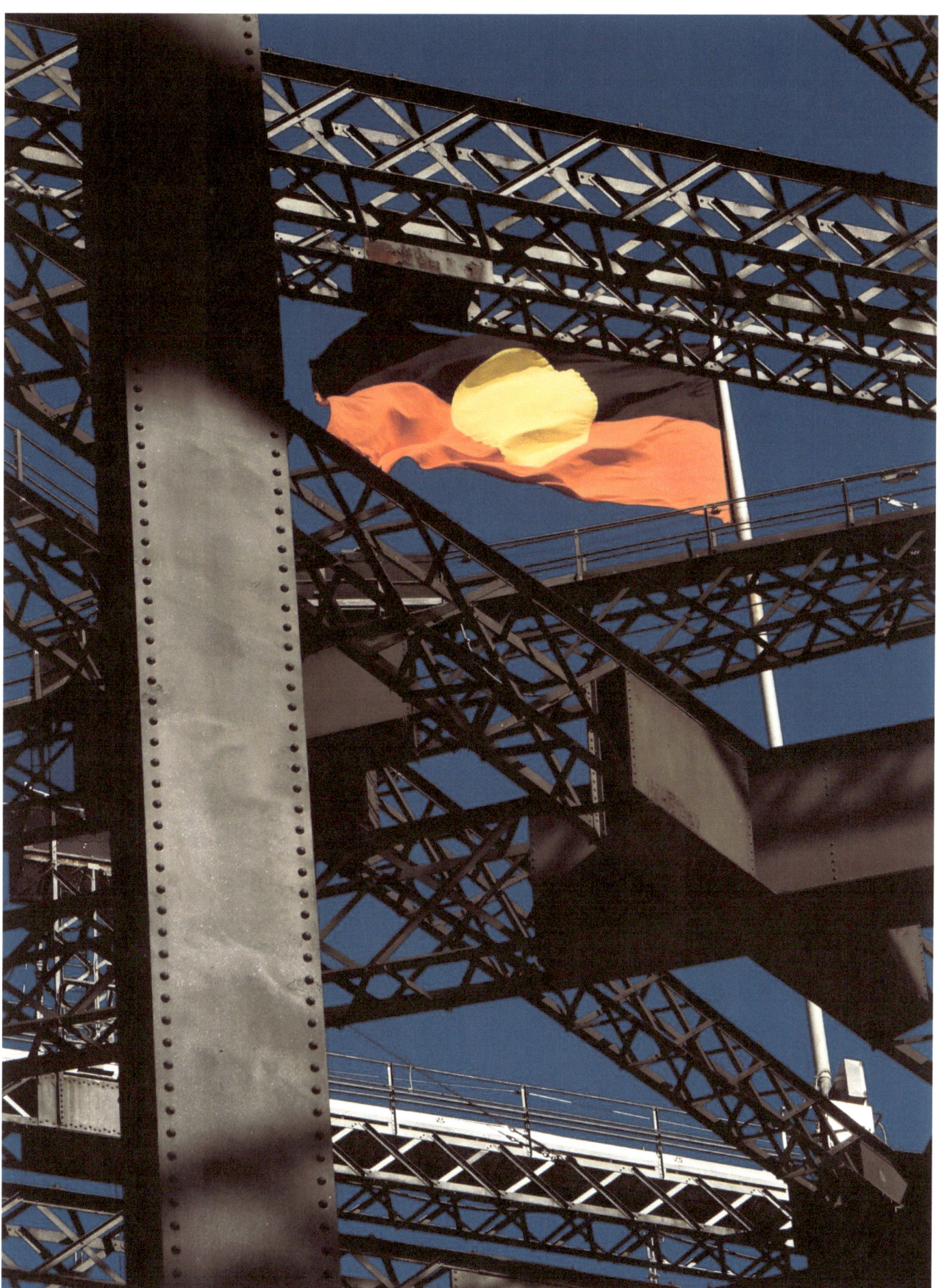

Australian Aborigine Flag – Karin Gottschalk

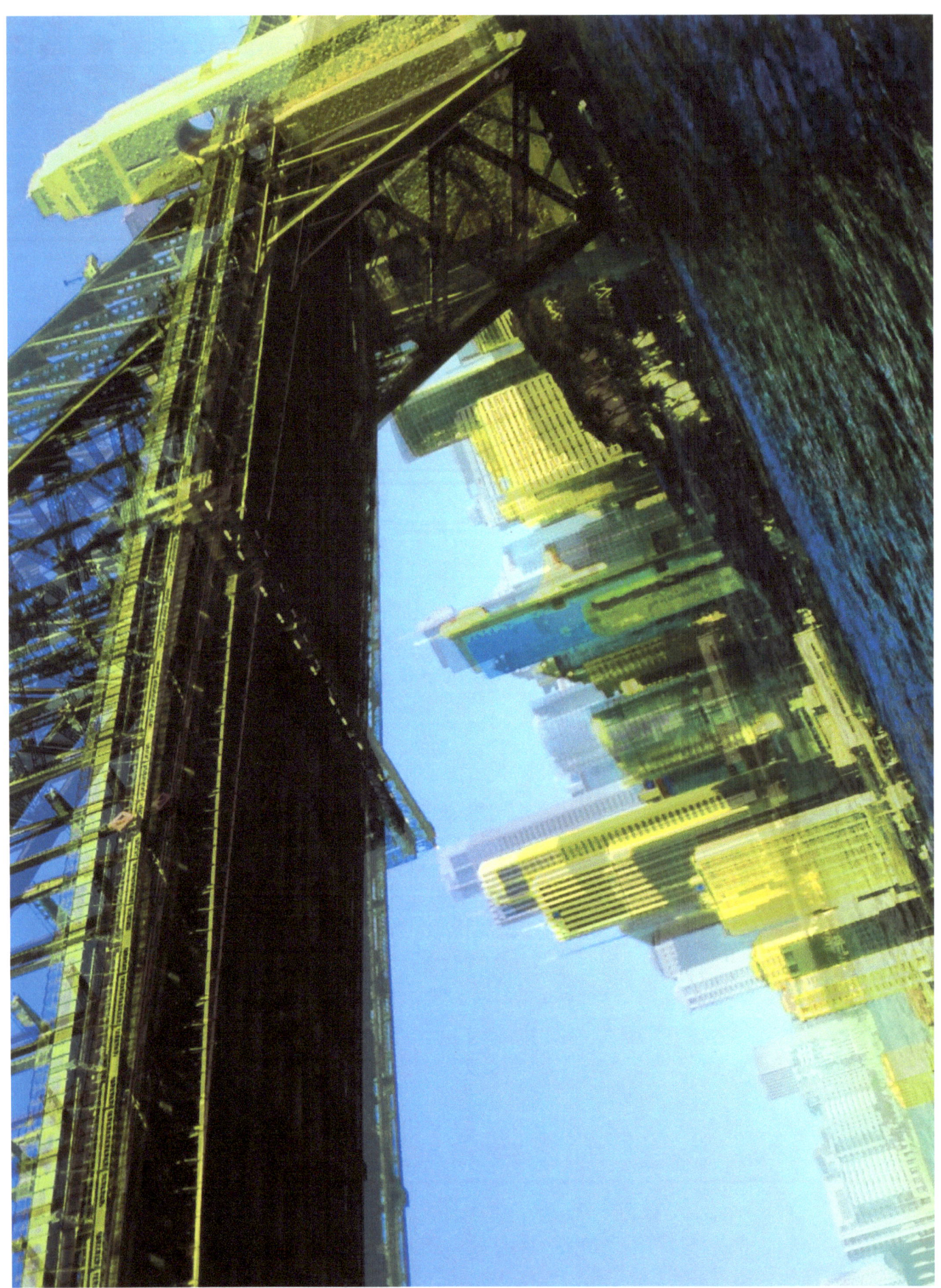

Feeling Tipsy ("We almost fell off the Wine Tasting cruiser") – Mark Plower

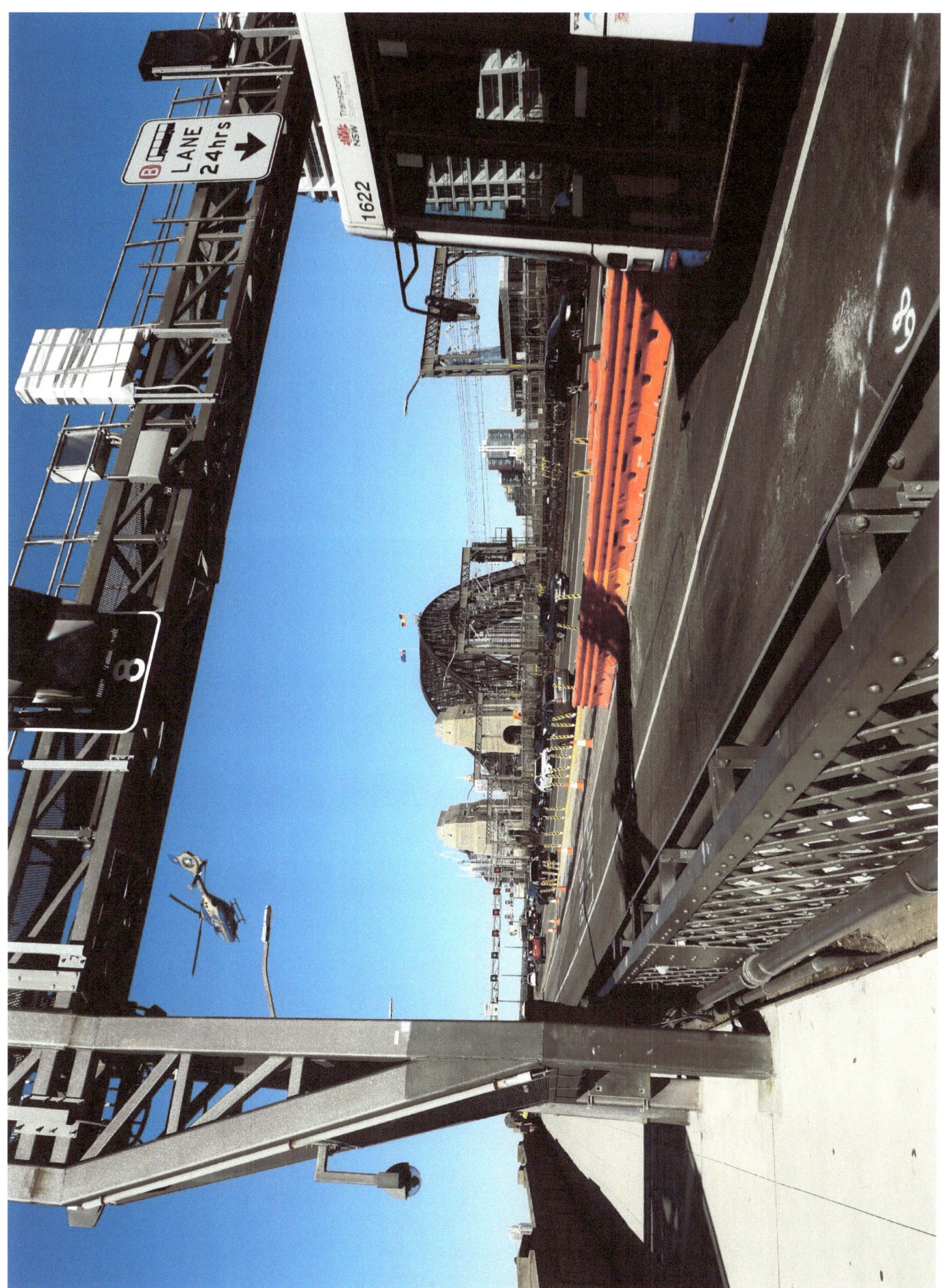

Bridge Approach from North Sydney – Brian Mackie

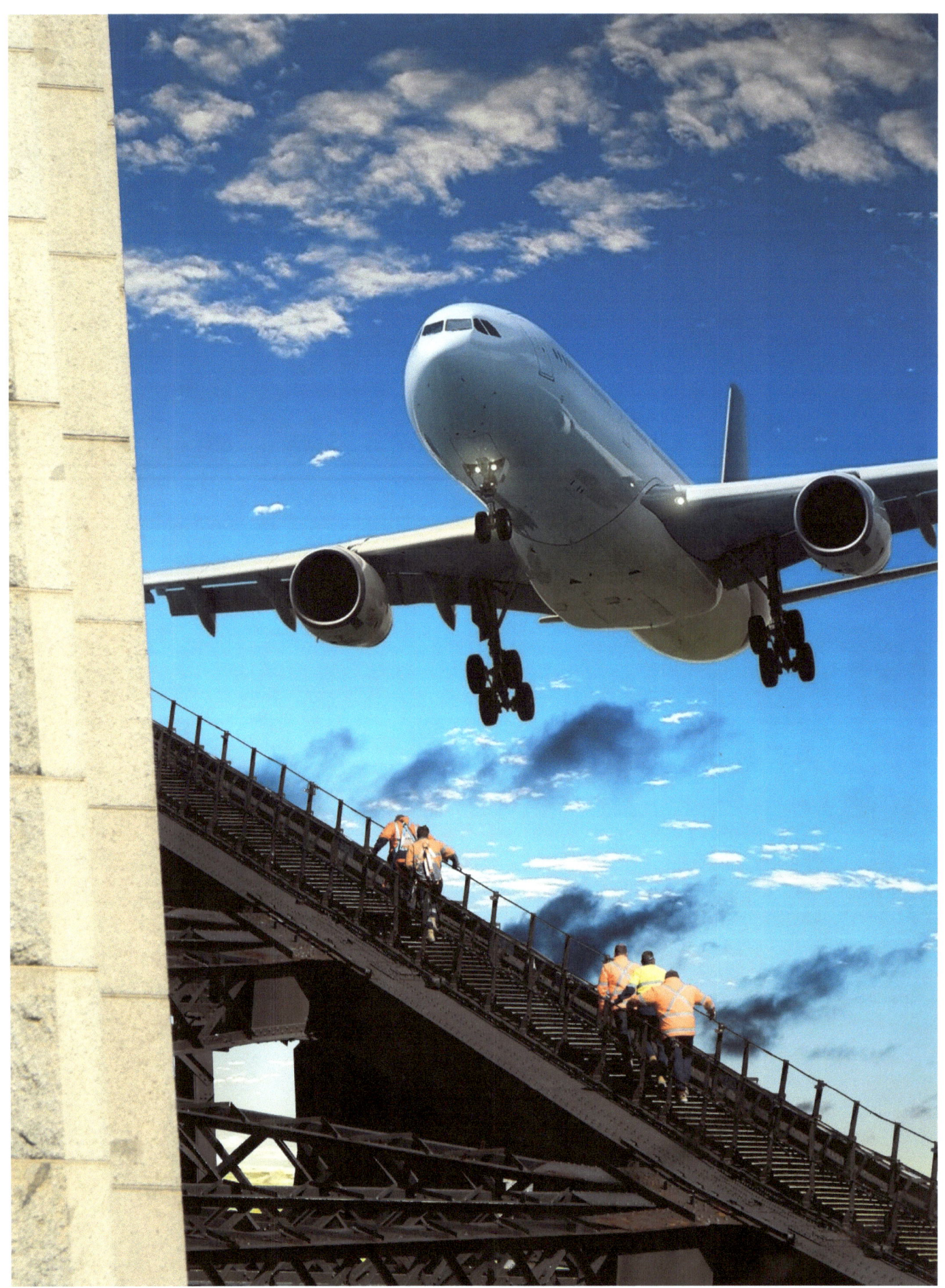

Bridge Walkers – Karin Gottschalk

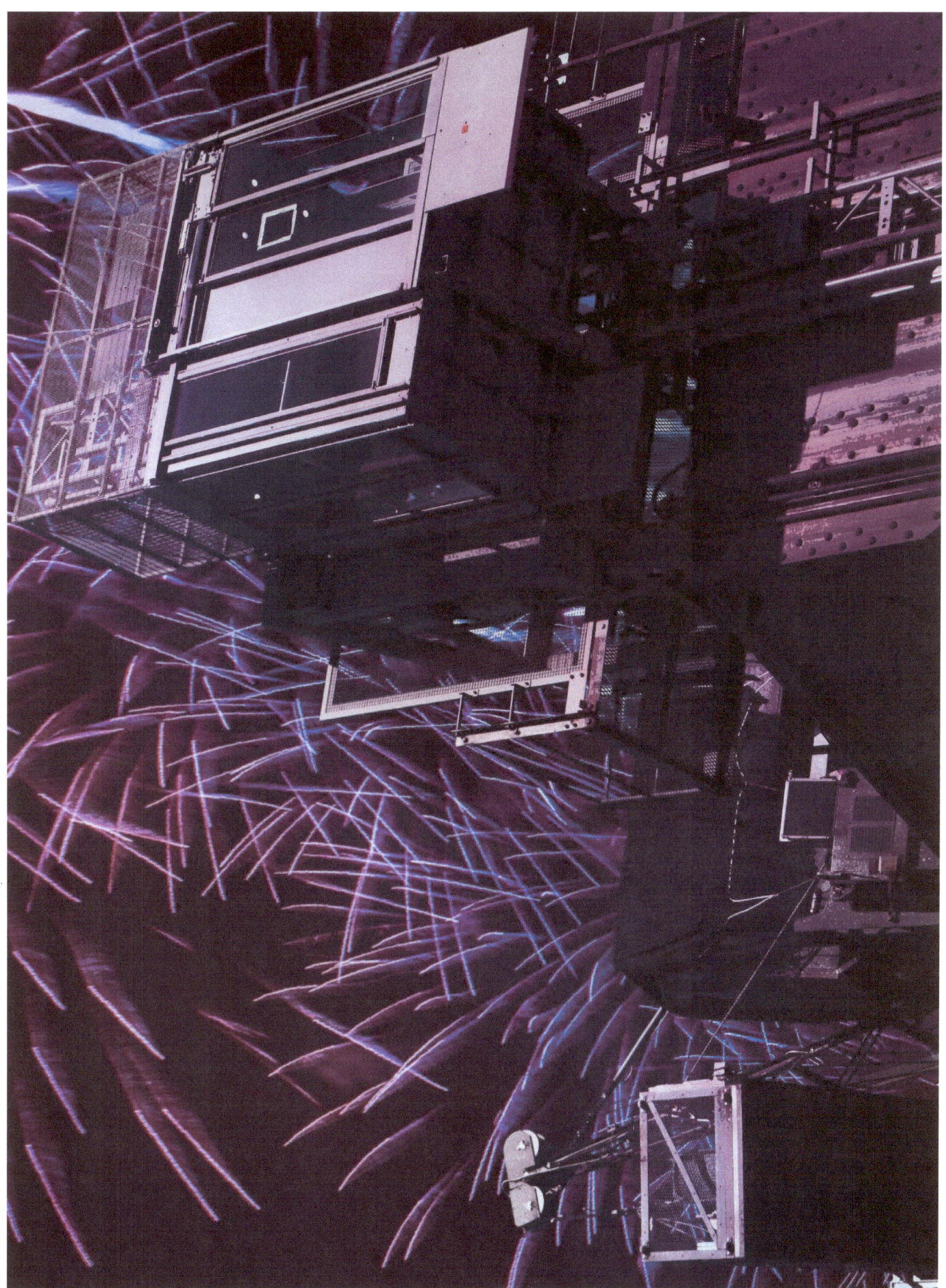
Fireworks over the Bridge Service Elevator – Carmel Morris

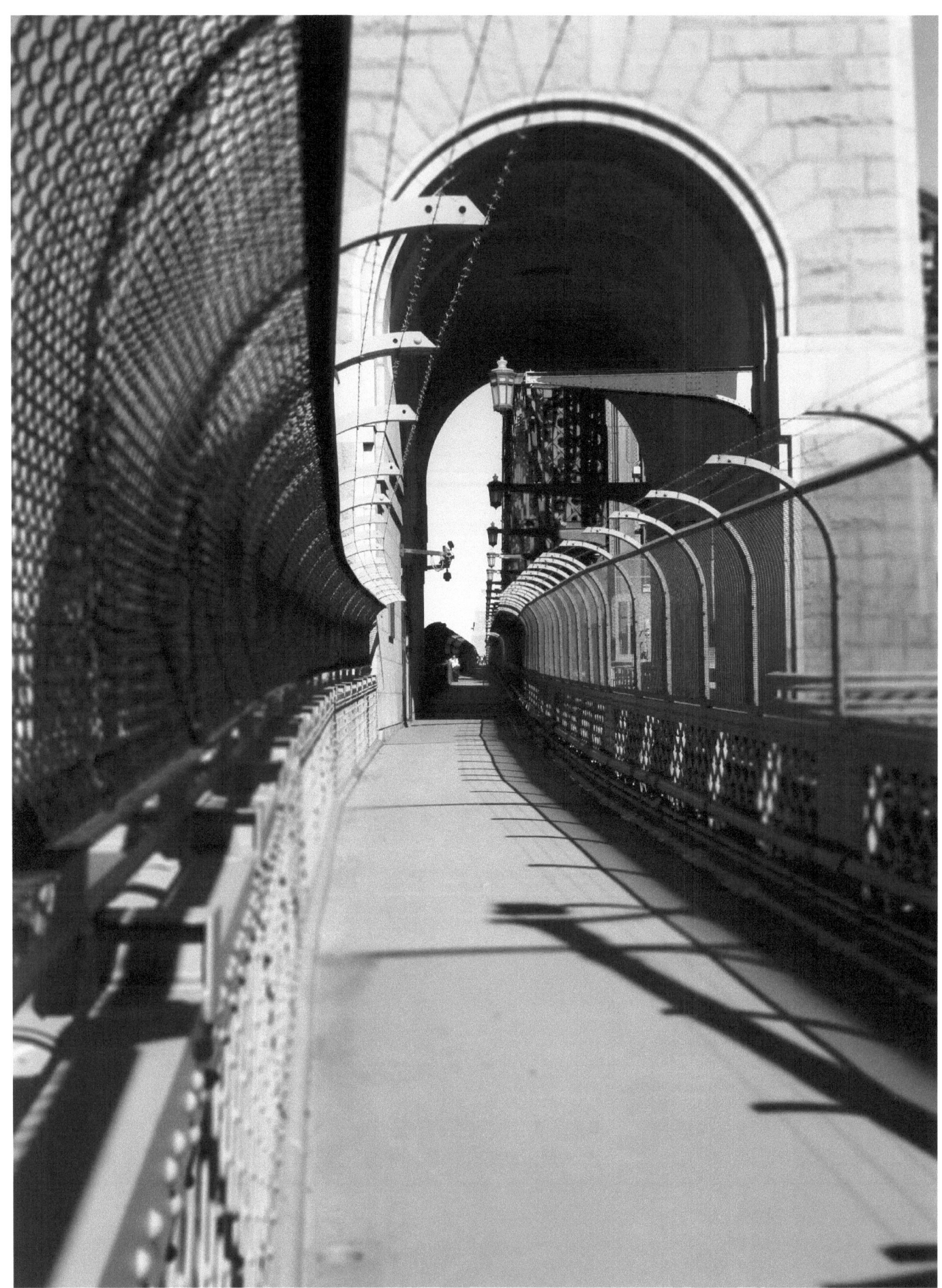

Pedestrian Walk – Eric Shipley

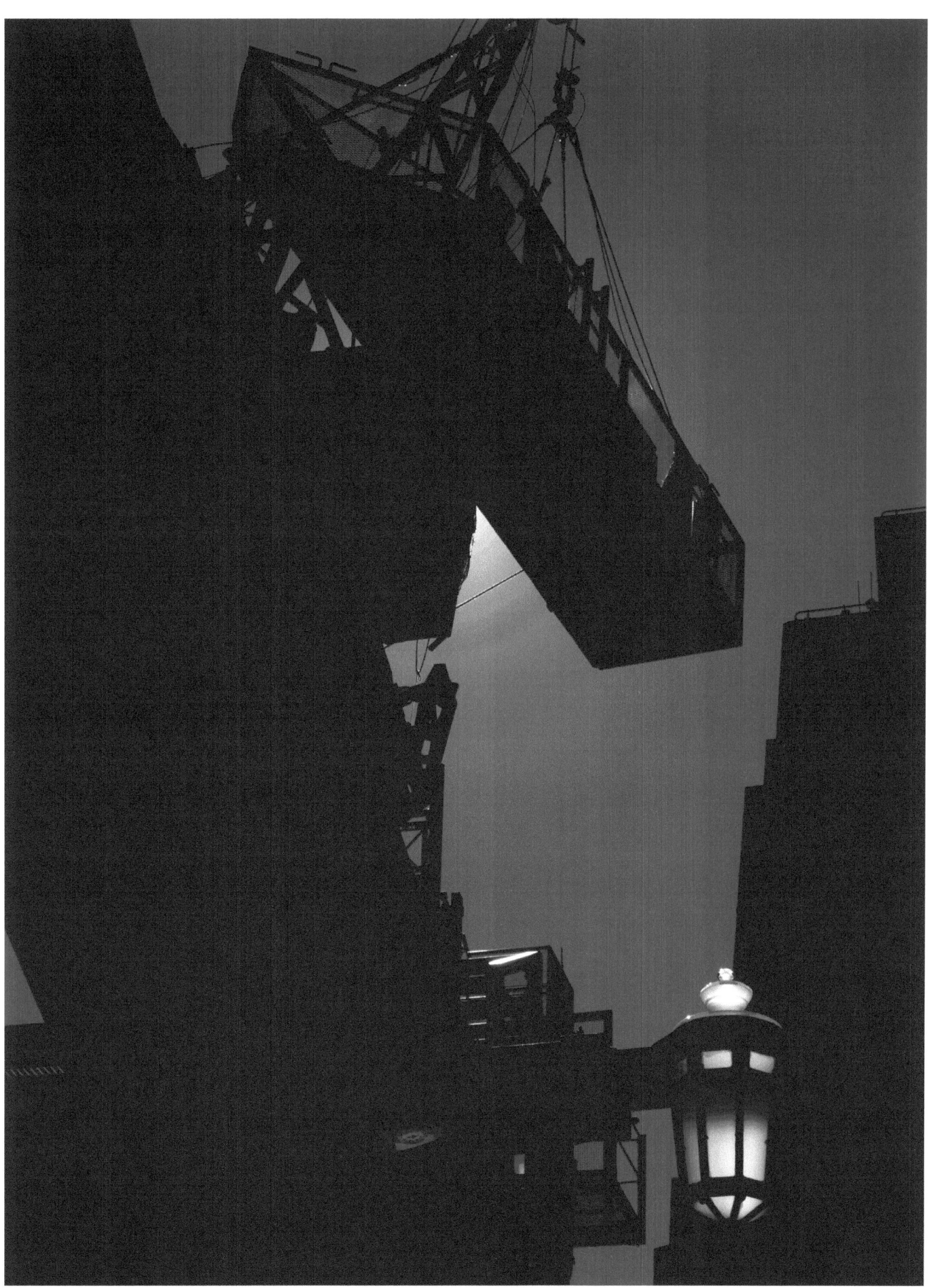

Maintenance Equipment – Peter Mackie

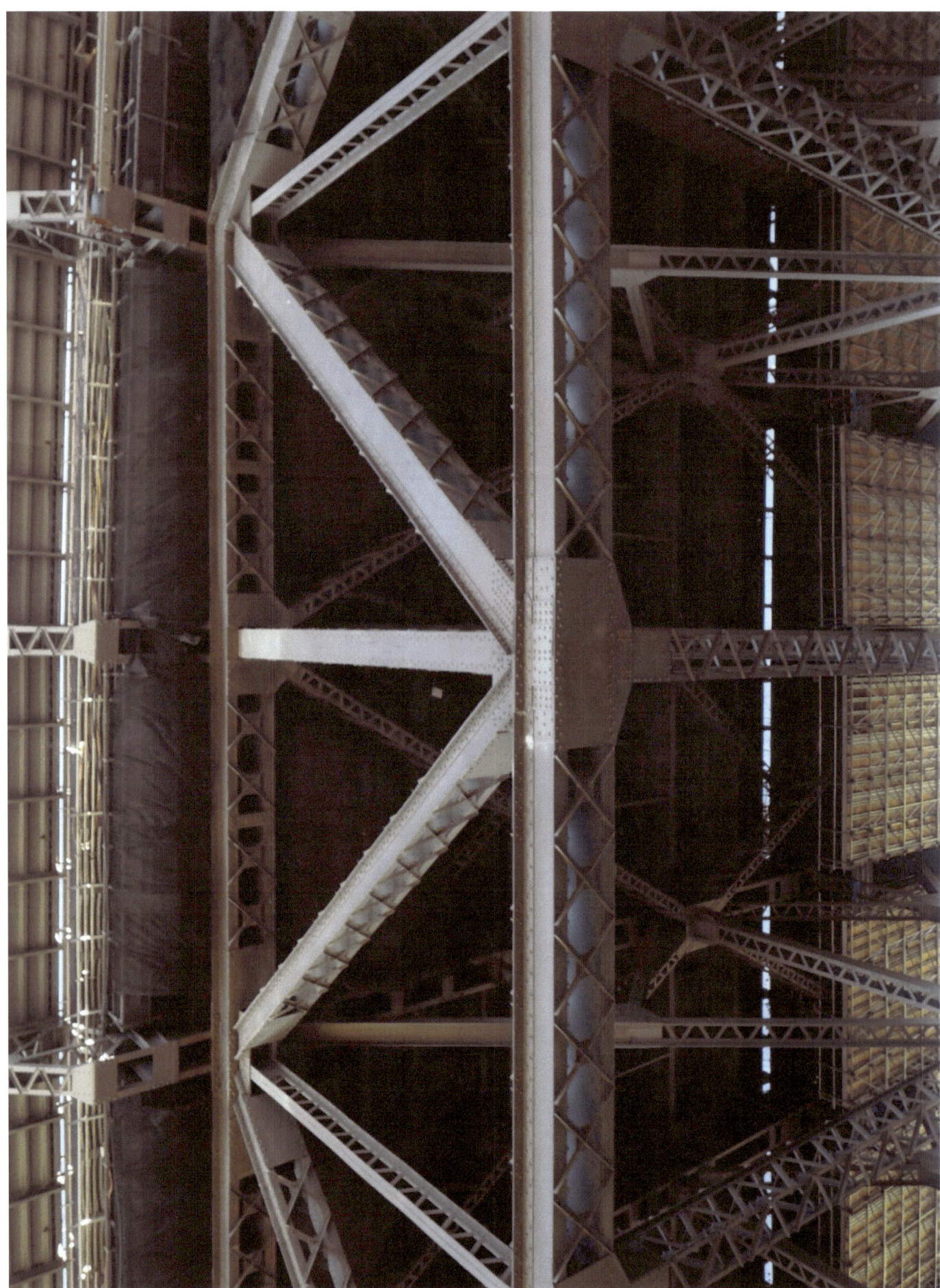

Under the Bridge – Petra Newman

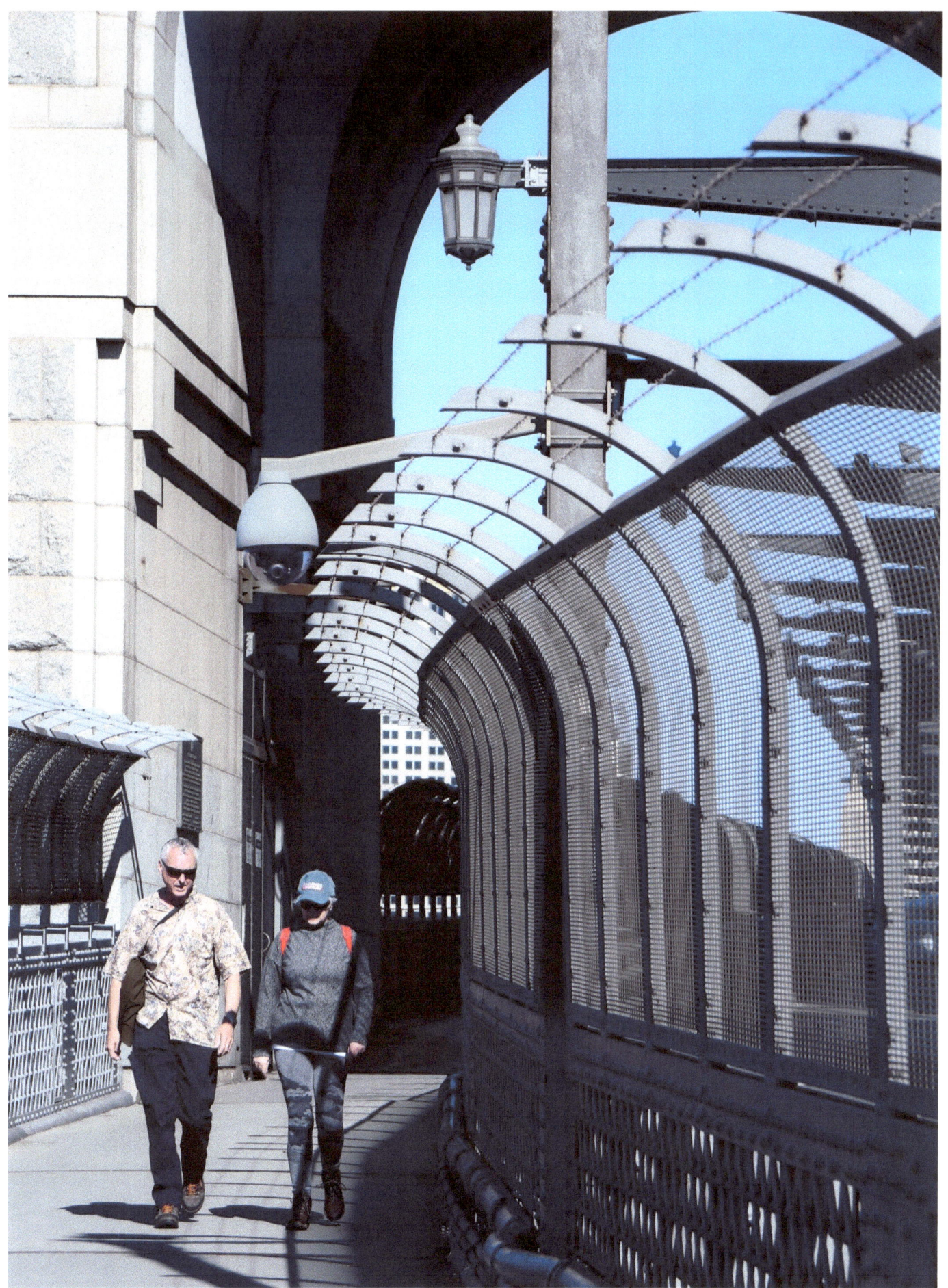

A Leisurely Bridge Stroll – Petra Newman

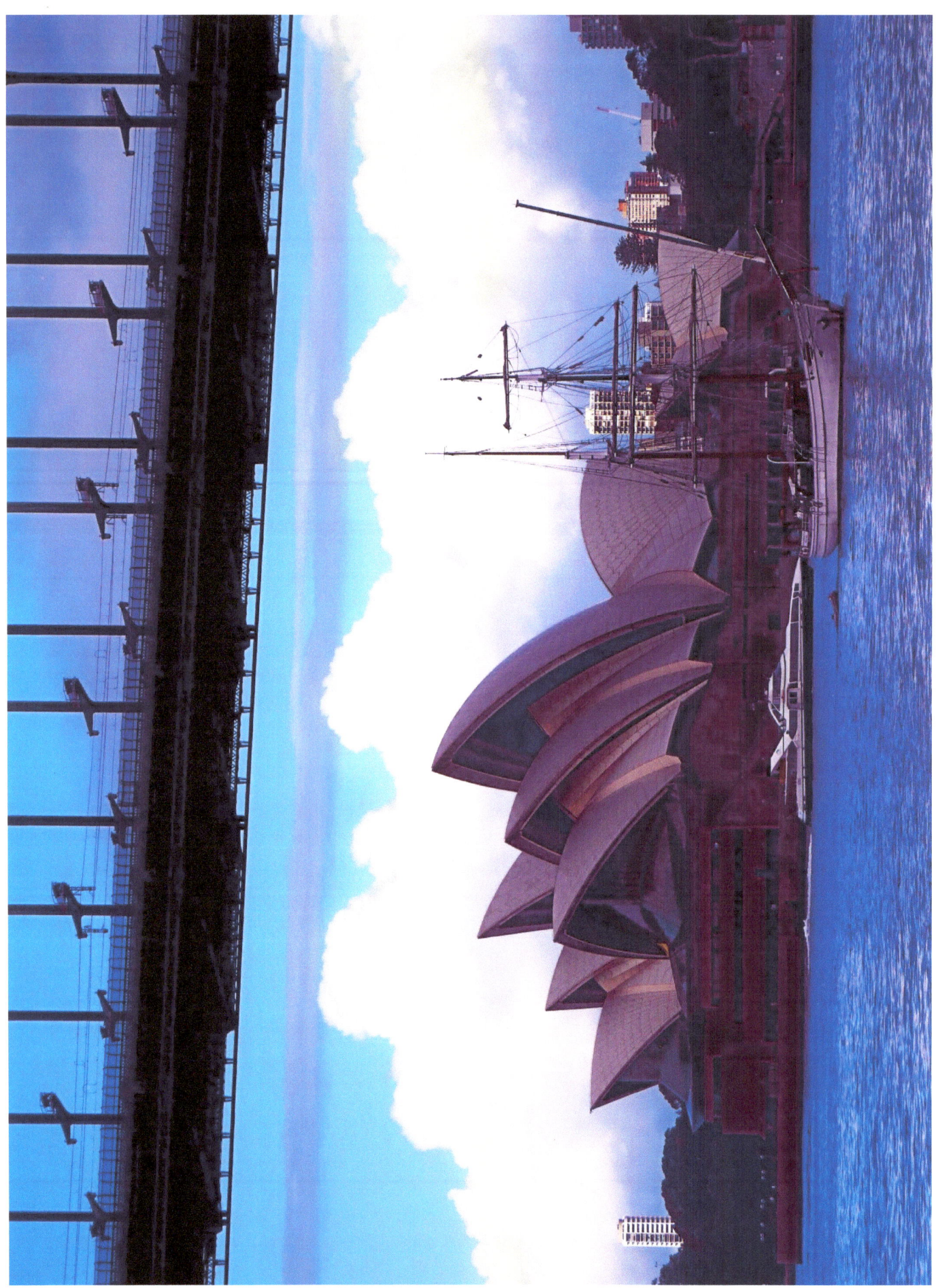

Winter Clouds Approach – Charlie Parker

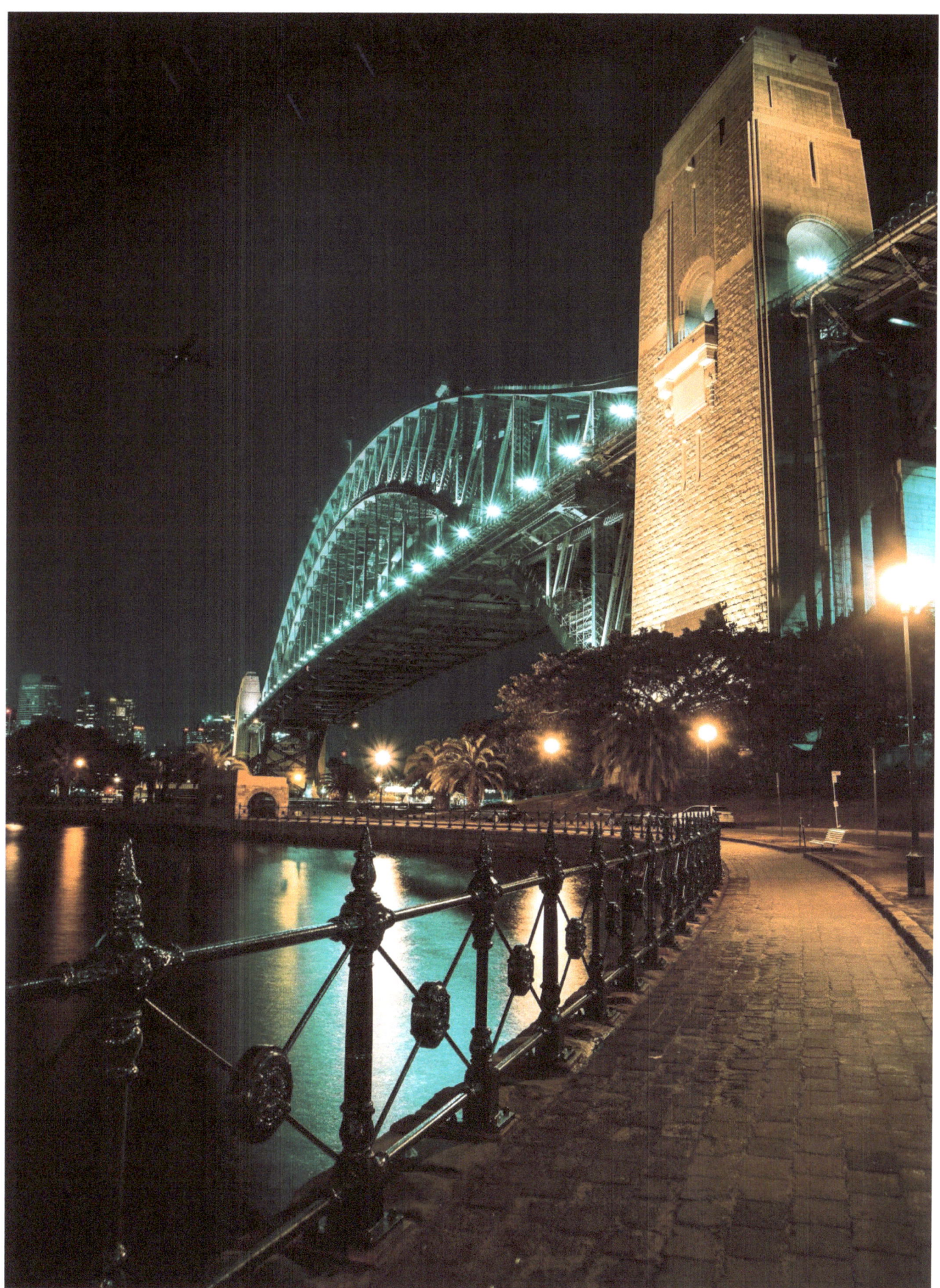

Night View from Milsons Point – Rijan Hamidovic

First published by Photality Graphics 2021
Copyright Photality 2021
George Street Sydney NSW 2000
All images modified to suit book format, color and aspect.

www.ingramcontent.com/pod-product-compliance
Lightning Source LLC
Chambersburg PA
CBHW051823210526
45473CB00005B/1719